3-

# BIRD
# AMBULANCE

*Eeny, Meeny, Miney*

# ARLINE THOMAS

# *BIRD*

# *AMBULANCE*

ILLUSTRATED WITH PHOTOGRAPHS:
CONVERSIONS BY JOSEPH STANLEY

CHARLES SCRIBNER'S SONS
*New York*

PRINTED IN THE UNITED STATES OF AMERICA
Library of Congress Catalog Card Number 77-140775

*TO THE BIRDS*

*AND THEIR PROTECTORS*

## ⟁ *Acknowledgments*

Grateful acknowledgment is made to Miss Jeanne Goodwin of the National Audubon Society for her help with research in connection with this book, to Miss Grace Davall and George Scott of the New York Zoological Society for advice on bird care, and to Dr. Leo Karmin, veterinarian, for his aid with my problem patients. For permission to reproduce photographs, I wish to thank Clarence Hutchenrider (pages 2, 74), Henry Kemp (pages 94, 102, 110, 127), and the *Long Island Press* (page 84).

#  Contents

# ~ *Illustrations*

*xi*

# 1

## I START A BIRD SHELTER

# 1. I Start a Bird Shelter

ANSWERING emergency calls about injured wild birds is part of my daily life. My "ambulance"—which is only a cardboard carton—carries a variety of patients that sometimes become fascinating friends. Many of them are young birds, but one was an old acquaintance that literally dragged itself to the door.

That happened the first year that my husband and I moved into a cottage built in the remnant of an oak forest in the Holliswood area of Long Island. Luckily for the birds and the local birdwatchers, many of these old trees still stand. As soon as we got our house in order, we set up a feeding station that brought the wild birds to our yard, some of them species I had never seen before. Armed with a copy of the bird-watcher's bible, Roger Tory Peterson's *Field Guide to the Birds,* I tried to identify as many as possible by their color, shape, and size. Later, when I got a pair of binoculars for my birthday, I went all out for bird-watching.

This sport, which has been called a benign and delightful madness, has gripped some ten million Americans. It is carried on for the pleasure of looking at birds in the wild and trying to learn

3

*The flight room*

their names. Boy Scouts go in for it as part of their training, but so do many other people. They cruise the roads, scan the lakes, tramp the woods, and keep records of the different birds they see. One banker arranges his business in distant cities so that he will be there at the best time for watching warblers, shore birds, or ducks. Housewives, more confined, keep lists of the birds they see in their yards, and some, like myself, become very fond of an individual bird that comes regularly to their feeders.

That first fall, I identified and made friends with a white-breasted nuthatch. The nuthatch gets its name from a family habit of pushing seeds and nuts into crevices where it splits, or "hatches," them with its beak. I could always recognize this bird because he was blind in one eye, which may have been the reason he came to me daily for food. Aside from his bad eye, Hatch was a handsome little fellow with a shiny black cap, gray back, and slender bill. All through the winter I saw him hitching up and down the trees in the garden, hunting insects in the bark; every morning he came to the window and called "Ank, Ank" for sunflower seeds and peanuts. Then one day in early spring he disappeared.

A week later, going out the door, I thought I saw a mouse crawling across the lawn toward me. Feeble "anks" helped me recognize my one-eyed Hatch, trailing an injured wing. Carrying him indoors, I gave him food and water. Afterward I put him in a big cardboard carton and covered the top with my garden sieve. On nice days I put this makeshift cage out on an open terrace, which has since been glassed in to provide a flight room for convalescing birds.

To make Hatch feel at home, my husband scattered leaves in the box and gave him an old fireplace log to climb on. Then Hatch went to work. All day long he whittled the rotting wood with his bill until he chipped out three holes—the size of a sunflower seed, of a shelled peanut, and of an unshelled nut. When I put seeds and nuts in his dish, he quickly hid them under the leaves. As he

*4*

got hungry, he pulled one out, wedged it into the proper hollow, and split the kernel into bite-size pieces. Once I put some nuts in the hole of his log but he indignantly yanked them out. Then he laid them carefully in a far corner, as if to let me know the log wasn't a pantry, but a table—to be set only at mealtimes. As long as he lived, my husband, who was an amateur craftsman himself, kept that log to show what a bird with a woodworking hobby could do.

In about three weeks, Hatch was able to fly around the kitchen. Then one sunny day, I took him outside and watched him zoom happily off to his favorite oak.

Though the nuthatch came to me by himself, I now get many injured birds because of my work with the National Audubon Society. This society was founded in 1886 by the American sportsman and ethnologist George Bird Grinnell and named in honor of John James Audubon (1785-1851) whose paintings of American birds in their native habitats have seldom been equaled. From its beginning, the organization has played a vital part in arousing the American public to the loss of our native birds and in working for protective legislation.

Its many members, in every state and from all walks of life, are concerned not only with the protection of birds but with the conservation of America's soil, water, forests, and all wildlife. In some states Audubon wardens patrol miles of bird sanctuaries; at times these wardens have given their lives to protect their charges. In schools throughout the country, the society sponsors and supports Audubon Junior Clubs that teach the need of environmental protection. Its lecturers tour some two hundred cities every year. At Audubon summer camps teachers and Scout leaders attend courses on the best way to educate man regarding his relationship with, and his place within, the natural ecological system.

At its national headquarters in New York City, the society often gets calls from bewildered people about individual birds in trouble. In any big city, birds do get into all sorts of trouble. Passing over the downtown section of Manhattan, a ruby-throated hummingbird blundered through a window on the thirty-sixth floor of an insurance building, bumped into a file cabinet, and injured a wing. One hot day a tired whippoorwill took refuge in a Fifth Avenue china shop, settling down among a group of porcelain figurines. Not until it began to preen itself did a startled salesman realize it was not part of his display. Birds fly head on into New York's skyscrapers and are stunned; unless rescued and given proper care, they are almost sure to die.

In the suburbs too birds come up against the hazards of our civilization. Starlings build nests in air conditioners and have to be evicted. Sparrows and finches take up housekeeping in rolled-up awnings; when the awning is lowered their brood is shunted to the pavement. Birds flounder into swimming pools, get hit by cars, and fly against overhead wires. When they are mauled by cats, the wounds often prove fatal unless antibiotics can be provided to ward off septicemia. Owls hide in garages, shore birds get fouled by oil slicks, and always and forever baby birds fall out of nests.

As part of its service, the Audubon Society has set up a volunteer bird-saving corps made up of members living in and around New York City. The work, which requires a knowledge of first aid and of wild birds, was started because most animal shelters are unable to give birds the special foods and protracted care they often need. The corps had an informal beginning. Members from nearby suburbs often phoned the society headquarters to learn what to do for injured birds they had found or that were brought to them. Eventually the staff asked some of these members to continue the work. Now when local animal shelters suggest that suburbanites contact Audubon headquarters about helpless birds they have found, the society refers to them to a volunteer in their neighborhood.

After serving an apprenticeship nursing home-town birds, I became an Audubon volunteer; soon even the local newspapers had my phone number which they give out in response to frantic calls from people who have found an injured wild bird and want to help it. As a result of a letter of recommendation from the National Audubon Society to the proper agencies, I was issued the required licenses from the state and federal governments to handle sick or injured birds, but I have no diploma in bird medicine. Luckily I can count on help from a local veterinarian.

Wild-bird care is a combination of common sense and know-how. However, a novice finds little help in books, since few have been written on this subject. This may be due to the fact that you are likely to be breaking a state or federal law if you harbor wild birds without a permit, something I did not know at first.

In the beginning when my know-how was very scant, I often turned for help to George Scott, for years head of the bird department at the Bronx Zoo. (This zoo, the finest and most progressive in the East, is under the direction of the New York Zoological Society whose research in the care of wildlife has been outstanding.)

Kindly Mr. Scott was always patience itself when I brought him my problems. He showed me how to "gentle" an injured bird to keep it from hurting itself further when handled. From him I also learned how to distinguish a sprained wing from a broken one and the best way to handle simple fractures. With hundreds of rare and exotic birds under his care, he was never too busy to help the humblest sparrow.

One rainy morning I arrived at the zoo with a yellow-shafted flicker I was worried about. This colorful member of the woodpecker family is designated by more than a hundred vernacular names—highhold, yellow-hammer, golden-wing, wake-up, and hairy wicket being a few. Flickers often feed on the ground and are particularly fond of ants. Driving their long bills into the burrows, they extend their whip-like, sticky tongues into them and pull them out loaded with ants.

My patient had arrived in a state of shock caused by flying against a window; when he came to he wouldn't eat any of the usual bird formulas I offered. At my wit's end to keep him from starving, I gave him a crumbled butter cookie. To my surprise he ate it. From then on, he lived mostly on cookies, but unfortunately they were too rich for him and brought on a stomach ailment.

Scotty listened to my story in his office behind the bird house. Then he carefully examined the bird's droppings.

"Rhubarb and soda three times a day," he advised. "Scald some chopped beef with boiling water and make him eat it—even if you have to feed him by force."

Back home, the flicker dutifully took his medicine from an eye dropper and, with a little persuasion, some beef. But deprived of his favorite cookies, he sat glumly in his cage. Suddenly to the consternation of us both, he began to burp. Open-mouthed, the bird stared accusingly at me, then furiously stropped his beak, perhaps to get rid of the commotion in his stomach. He kept it up, alternately burping and stropping, until he was relieved of his indigestion.

When his stomach trouble seemed entirely cured, I put him outside with the other flickers that in the spring spend their time raiding the neighborhood anthills.

# 2 〜

## OWL QUARTET — AND ONE MORE

*Jersey*

# 2. Owl Quartet—and One More

THE success with my first patient, the nuthatch, made me something of a local celebrity. Pessimistic about any wild bird's survival in captivity, my neighbors had said, "They always die after a few days."

Hatch's recovery amazed them, and soon they were asking me all sorts of questions about bird care, few of which I could answer. But when I learned that they usually fed injured wild birds (insect eaters and others) only bread and water or bread and milk, it struck me that it might have been this scanty diet as much as their injuries that had "done them in." Of course it was pure luck that I had learned something about Hatch's food habits before he was hurt.

Although bread is a handy supplement, birds need more nourishing food for a long convalescence and to try to raise baby birds solely on bread and milk is to court disaster. Yet every summer I get several undersized, scrubby-looking fledglings that well-meaning samaritans have tried to raise on this deficiency formula. These youngsters are usually poorly feathered, too weak to fly, and their feet and joints are often enlarged; actually they are suffering from a form of gout. Robert Stroud, who wrote the authoritative *Digest on the Diseases of Birds* while in prison (and whose tragic life was the subject of the book and film *Bird Man of Alcatraz),* found by experiment that he could produce gout in canaries by feeding them exclusively on bread and milk. Milk may be a perfect food for people, but not for birds.

The month after I had released Hatch my undeserved reputation as a bird expert brought me two more casualties: a red-winged blackbird and a wood thrush, both too far gone to be patched up. Then came my owl initiation, which began with three babies. (Until then my acquaintance with these birds had been limited to Hallowe'en decorations.)

A tall tree in our area with a large hole in its trunk made an ideal owl home—especially since it was within easy flying distance of a stable. Here, rumor had it, mice were often seen, and judging from the pellets of mice bones under their tree, the owls were good hunters. The young owls had been harried and hauled from their nest in the tree by a flock of screaming jays. Plopping almost sixty feet to the ground, they were so badly winded it was touch and go for a while whether they would live. As they crouched in their shoebox ambulance, they were three shapeless lumps of feathers, punctuated by round, yellow eyes. As if their outsized beaks were too heavy for them, they hung their heads. Their feathered eartufts, as well as their size, identified them as screech owls, a bird that has the distinction of coming in either of two colors: red-brown or gray. This color difference is found in both male and female screech owls regardless of age or season of the year. Of my three, one was reddish, the other two gray.

Deciding to put the little owls in a larger carton, I reached for the reddish one, which was also the smallest. (The mother owl lays her eggs two or three days apart but begins to brood them the very first day. So when the last egg is laid, the first is already partly incubated, which makes for different-sized young in the same nest.) He backed away and snapped his beak. Just guessing at his sex, I named him Snapper.

After consulting the Zoo, I offered them all some raw hamburger. Snapper and the middle-sized one looked bewildered at this substitute for their mouse-grasshopper diet, but the largest one scrambled over to me and began eating out of my hand. Known from then on as Wimpy, he turned out to be a lovable extrovert and the leader of the gang. Though normally nocturnal, the youngsters quickly got used to a daytime schedule, thriving on three meals of raw beef. At night they slept quietly in their carton.

Mornings, after spreading newspapers, I let them loose in the kitchen. Like three little gnomes, they toured the room. Exploring the furniture, Wimpy blinked in wide-eyed surprise when the garbage-can lid snapped. After a while they grew bold enough to run and skip, waving their stumpy wings in flight practice. Snapper often slipped and fell on his face, then, gravely righting himself, slowed down to a toddle. Soon they could flutter to the chair backs and later to the windowsill. From there their keen eyes watched the affairs of the neighborhood. Contrary to widespread belief, owls are certainly not blind in daylight. In fact, they see very well, but most see better at dusk because their eyes, adapted for night hunting, are so sensitive that the iris almost closes in strong light. In addition, the eye of an owl, like that of the hawk, can be instantly focused to see either near or far; it is probably the most efficient organ of vision in the world.

Watching an airplane overhead or an animal in the street, my owls would crane their necks and swivel their heads until they looked straight back over their shoulders. Then—a trick that often alarmed me—they would snap their heads frontward so fast that it seemed as though they had turned them in a complete circle. This was only an illusion, but the movement, made easy by their fourteen neckbones against our seven, is responsible for the old folk tale that

*13*

the sure way to kill an owl is to walk around and around it—as it keeps twisting its head to follow you, it will soon wring its own neck.

Scientists, who say birds are ruled solely by instinct, caution us not to attribute human emotions to them. But as I got to know them better, I became convinced that owls, more than any others, are an exception. A blend of monkey and winged cat, screech owls can take on almost any expression by a shift of their feathery eartufts. Once I accidentally hit Snapper on the head. He hunched his shoulders, eyes glaring, feathers bristling, while he flicked his eartufts into a pair of devilish horns. It took little imagination to believe he was swearing at me.

While I was getting some firsthand knowledge about owls, Simone, a friend from Paris, visited me. Fascinated by the birds, she offered to help me care for them. As a reward, she was allowed to name the middle-sized one. Touching his head lightly with a drop of perfume, she translated his family name (owl) into French, calling him Hibou.

And such is the magic of words—and owls—that Hibou really seemed French. Like all of his kin, he had a nearly human face. Rings of short flattened feathers formed a "face" for his round eyes. His beak, bordered by a silky mustache, was very like a nose. But his flexible eartufts, which he often held at a rakish angle, gave him his personality. Simone assured me he needed only a white boutonniere on his gray shoulder to complete the illusion of a jaunty boulevardier.

"Look at him, my gallant Hibou," she called to me once. "See how he takes care to sheathe his talons when I hold him on my finger." Tickled silly by all the attention, the rascal flattened his eartufts, a picture of demure sweetness as he coyly bent his head sideways.

Simone spoiled him terribly, often taking him out of the cage and whispering endearments in French to him. She also fed him bits of feathered skin, which she scissored from the chicken heads that were part of his diet. Like all birds of prey, he had to have either fur or feathers in his diet to stimulate his digestion and clean out his stomach. Some hours after this meal, he spit up an oval pellet, consisting of feathers with any indigestible matter neatly wrapped inside.

For days after Simone left, Hibou seemed to listen for her footsteps, turning expectantly toward the doorway through which she no longer appeared. He moped, too, even neglecting his fastidious preening. *"Tu es drôle, mon petit,"* I ventured, hoping to cheer him. Droll or not, Hibou evidently knew how French should sound; he almost clawed a hole in the window screen to escape my fractured accent. But, finally, with a *c'est la vie* attitude worthy of his Gallic name, he resigned himself to his loss and took an interest in his feathers again.

Although Hibou was never as friendly with me as he was with Simone, all the birds became quite tame. Even Snapper flew readily to me. Wimpy, the gregarious show-off, often rode around the house perched on my shoulder. He was just as amiable with the neighborhood children who loved to drop in and see the owls. Looking like a character from a Disney film, Wimpy fluffed his feathers and perched on their fingers, waiting expectantly to be petted.

One morning, however, alone on the window, he reverted. He was looking out into the yard when a dog dashed around the corner and frightened him. In a flash his chubby face and body lengthened into a thin, vertical line while his eartufts shot straight up in the air. Narrowing his eyes to slits, he stood frozen like a statue, the irregular pattern of his barred feathers making him look like a tree branch. In the woods, against the bark of a tree, he would have been invisible, a perfect example of nature's camouflage. But his sudden and eerie transformation in the kitchen sent chills along my spine; it was as though some awesome primeval force from the deep forest had slipped into the room and taken possession of him.

# BIRD AMBULANCE

While the owls were very young, they neeeded no water to drink. But later, one hot day, I put some in a shallow pan on the floor. As curious as monkeys, they glided down from the sill and peered over the rim. Steeling himself to get up his courage, Wimpy took a long drink, letting the water slowly trickle down his throat like rare wine. Reassured, Hibou and Snapper did the same. Finally Wimpy stepped into the pan. Astounded at his own daring, he stood gazing at his submerged feet until, getting braver, he sat down on the water and dunked his tail. Ruffling his feathers, he began to bathe, flailing his wings and dipping his face until his fluffy plumage was sodden, thereby revealing an unbelievably skinny neck and legs. According to experts, Wimpy was merely following the behavior pattern for bathing that came to him from his ancestors. In any case, he was thoroughly wet.

Hibou tried next, repeating Wimpy's vigorous actions and scattering still more water on the floor, which left an almost empty pan for Snapper. Recklessly he threw himself on his face and slid his breast along the bottom, trying to scoop up as much moisture as he could. Then keeling over sideways, he attempted to wet first one wing and then the other, until he lost his balance and rolled out onto the floor.

Once, this fondness for bathing brought Wimpy to the brink of disaster. At lunchtime, unmindful of the birds, I began heating a pan of water for tea. As it started to bubble, Wimpy sailed through the air, headed for a steaming bath. Swinging wildly, I slapped him away, just in time to save him from becoming a boiled owl. He dropped to the floor and stalked off, seemingly annoyed because he had been cheated out of his dip.

As frolicsome as kittens, the owls loved to play. One of the games was "Pounce," a preparation for their role as hunters. By now they had lost their baby fluffiness; their wing feathers were firm and strong except at the edges, which would remain soft and downy all their lives. This is a characteristic of all owls that lets them fly in ghostlike silence and drop quietly down on their prey. Understandably, the Indian name for owl means "hush-wing." The game went something like this. While the owls sat on a perch, I held out a feather. They waited until I let it fall, meanwhile swaying their heads like pendulums to focus their eyes. Gliding like shadows, they swooped, trying to clutch it with their flexible claws. When it drifted away, they chased it across the room, bumping their heads together and tumbling over one another, all the while whinnying with excitement. Even when they were older, they did not screech unpleasantly but gave a warbling *whoo-whoo* call. (The screeching screech owl is a European species.)

When the three owls were about half-grown, an acquaintance who was a naturalist asked me to take on another one. Rescued during a cloudburst in New Jersey, it had been leading a pampered but lonely life in his city apartment, living on white mice that cost fifty cents apiece. The newcomer, named Jersey, was about the size of Snapper, the small red owl, but his feathers were gray like those of the other two.

A meek little bird, Jersey never adjusted to the rowdy ways of my lively trio, yet he followed them around hoping to make friends. He often edged up to them and timidly fluttered his wings, but they either jumped on his head or stepped on his face. At feeding time too, they gave him no peace. A slow eater, Jersey liked to pause and look around between bites. Hurriedly bolting their own food, the others took turns snatching his away. Always treating him like a rank outsider, they never let him join in any owl games, except one in which he was "it."

I saw them start this one warm morning when they were all sitting on the windowsill staring outdoors, Wimpy at one end, Jersey the other. Turning his head, Wimpy nudged Hibou, who in turn pushed Snapper. Closing ranks, the three sidled along the sill. They pressed their bodies together at a crazy angle, leaning their combined weight against Jersey to squeeze him against the window frame until he began to pant. Finally, almost suffocated, he dropped to the floor and gazed up at his tormentors in puzzled innocence. Then, fairly chuckling with glee, they spread out again with plenty of room to spare.

Although more or less resigned to being pushed around, once when the going got too tough, Jersey tried to escape. Making a wild dive to the floor, he jumped headlong into the black border of the linoleum, mistaking it for a hole. Backing away, he tried again, this time banging his head against the wall. Baffled by his failure to find a hiding place, he walked slowly away, shaking his tail. That afternoon he disappeared, and though I looked everywhere in the house, I couldn't find him. I even searched the garden in the belief that, rejected by his peers, he had slipped out the door and run away. It was almost evening when I reached into a cabinet drawer and felt something soft. Pulling out the drawer, I found Jersey huddled in a corner behind my knife box. I stroked his head, gave him an extra large piece of meat to comfort him and put him back on the window with the rest. A few minutes later, he was crouching abjectly, while the others, walking back and forth along the sill, planted their feet squarely on his neck and clobbered him with their beaks.

After that, he rarely sat with them; instead he perched on the towel rack, where he watched me do my chores or stared at the wall. At night too, he kept apart from the rest, sitting on the lower of the two perches in their carton, while the others perched above him. Unfortunately, sleeping under three healthy owls left its mark on him—every morning I had to wash his head.

By midsummer the nearly grown birds were 10 inches tall and flying well. However, as often happens with birds that people raise, they were too tame to release in a residential neighborhood. The problem was solved when the Audubon Society proposed keeping them for the rest of the summer at their Greenwich, Connecticut, camp, where conservation courses are given to teachers, Scout leaders, and bird-lovers.

After the owls were settled in their new home I went to visit them. Kept in a picturesque red barn that had been converted into a nature museum, they were the only live exhibits there at the time. Groups of students gathered around their cage as the camp biologist discussed owls, food chains, and the primeval accident that some 400 million years ago resulted in the creation of green plants. Scribbled against a nearby boulder, my notes are a vivid reminder of my introduction to ecology.

Since most animals (birds included) eat only certain kinds and sizes of food, a plant-animal community can be broken down into separate food chains, a series of living things directly linked to one another by what they eat. The first link in a food chain is always a plant. With my birds as firsthand examples, the biologist discussed their rather simple food chain, which is seed-mouse-owl; the mouse eats the seeds to nourish its body and the owl lives on mice. The animals nearest the base of a food chain are necessarily more numerous than those at the top, making a sort of food pyramid. Ideally there should always be more mice than owls, otherwise these birds are forced to leave the community or resort to substitute foods such as grasshoppers or any other small animal they can catch.

Although the various food chains in the world differ in many ways, their make-up is the same. They all consist of green plants, herbivores, and carnivores. The individuals that make up the community may come and go—some are eaten, others are killed by accidents, and new ones are born. But the community remains much the same unless something upsets the balance of nature. It may be upset by floods, droughts, disease, or, worst of all, the unwise acts of man.

Upsetting this balance triggers a series of dangerous re-actions. Nature tries to restore it and overreacts. When farmers wipe out one pest with powerful chemicals, they soon find their crops afflicted with others that are resistant to the chemicals. The poison sprays also kill bees which are needed to pollinate the blossoms of fruit trees. If bees are killed, there will be less fruit. Worse, the impact of many of these poisons is vastly magnified in food chains. They often kill insect-eating birds that normally control the pests that destroy the farmers' crops, a domino theory that has many present-day scientists worried.

My four owls turned unusually solemn when the lecturer described their background, mentioning that in prehistoric times the cavemen believed owls to be the playmates of devils. The Romans, too, abhorred them, and when an owl perched in the Forum, the whole city went into mourning. In Egypt a pharaoh got rid of an official by simply sending him an owl's statue, an invitation to commit suicide. Only the Greeks considered the owl clan sacred and the special wards of Pallas Athena, the goddess of wisdom. As recently as fifty years ago, many people disliked owls, believing that they foraged on chickens and birds. Then scientists, studying their habits, found that owls—both the giant and midget varieties—helped maintain the balance of nature by eating immense quantities of harmful rodents and insects. After their praises had been sung for a while, the four birds began to preen themselves, as if they felt they had a right to be proud of their clan's good deeds.

As I approached their cage later, they recognized me and whimpered to be let out. When I opened the door they swarmed over me, while the campers ran for their cameras. Before all those enthusiastic camera fans, Wimpy tried to steal the show. On an old wagon wheel in front of the museum, a favorite prop for taking pictures, he mugged pose after pose, arranged his feathers, spread his wings, or turned his head for a profile shot. Undoubtedly he was the most photographed owl of the year, and he certainly seemed to enjoy the limelight.

Posed alone, Hibou and Snapper sat nicely. However, the four of them together were impossible. To keep them in position we attached cords to their legs and tethered them to a log but they immediately started frolicking and leapfrogging over each other. This kept me busy untangling their strings. Then, after roughing up Jersey, the others chased him out of camera range where he hid in the grass. The only recognizable picture I ever got of him was taken at home before he went to camp. I sat him on a row of books in a little mortarboard fashioned from a scrap of black paper and trimmed with a tassel made of sewing thread. Unfortunately he scrunched down, drawing his head in his shoulders, and looked more scared than scholarly.

While I was at camp, the biologist who had charge of the owls came over and talked to me about them. He had been teaching them to forage by letting them out every once in a while in a nearby field so they could learn to catch grasshoppers before their final release. Screech owls eat grasshoppers and moths all during their lifetime, and this hunting practice was to insure their survival in the wild.

"For an amateur, you did a good job raising them," he complimented. "They're healthy little birds and must have gotten a proper diet."

Although flattered by his praise, I was still concerned about my low bird on the totem pole, meek little Jersey. Almost afraid of his answer, I asked, "The smallest gray one, how's he getting along?"

"A whiz at hunting grasshoppers," he astounded me by saying, "and the only one so far to catch a mouse."

Like the parent of an underachiever who has suddenly made good, I glowed with pride.

Bird expert Roger Tory Peterson once theorized that women are likely to be more anthropomorphic about birds than men are and tend to regard them as little human beings dressed in feathers. In the case of another owl patient, I must plead guilty to the charge.

One evening an excited garage owner phoned to say that an owl had flown into his building during a snowstorm. He was afraid of it and wanted it removed. From the garbled description he gave, I could not tell what kind it was, except it did not have eartufts like a screech owl. Expecting anything from the great gray to the huge barred owl of the deep woods, I took heavy gauntlets to handle it.

Tiptoeing into the garage, I strained to get a look at the fierce unknown—then burst out laughing. There, sitting on a box, was our smallest eastern owl, a tiny saw-whet, named for its call: a soft, rasping "scree-kaw" somewhat like the sound made by filing a saw. A mouse hunter from Canada, this midget had probably come south looking for food, as saw-whets often do in winter, and had injured a wing.

At home, when I opened my ambulance, the little owl hopped out and tried to fly across the kitchen. However, his drooping wing would not support him, so he glided to the floor. Standing there like a brown-and-white elf, he drew himself up to his full height of 7 inches and gazed at me with quiet dignity. I named him Coco and for a month knew the charm of his owl personality.

Although baby owls should have three or four meals a day, Coco, as a grownup, needed only one. In late afternoon I fed him strips of raw beef. Holding the meat in one claw, he tore off small mouthfuls with his little hooked beak. Twice a week he got a chicken head to supply the needed roughage.

Until his wing drew back into place, I kept him caged; later I often let him fly around in the kitchen. Although at first he seemed reserved, I soon learned that he had a bump of curiosity bigger than he was. After skimming silently around the room, he usually perched on the curtain rod. From there he watched with intense interest everything I did; all my daily chores fascinated him and the time I baked a cake he got so excited he could hardly stand it.

Sitting on the rod, he stared in amazement as I laid out the ingredients, bobbing his head as owls do when I walked to and from the table. When I broke the eggs, he looked at me startled, as though surprised by a jack-in-the-box; his yellow eyes, always big, popped open even wider. Finally his curiosty got too much for him, and he flew down onto the towel rack to get a closer view of the goings on. I picked up a spoon and started to stir. With that his head, moving back and forth, seemed to jump from one shoulder to the other, as if disconnected from his body. At last, throwing caution aside, he flitted lightly over my head and perched on the edge of the mixing bowl like an inquisitive sprite.

If startled, Coco made a clicking sound with his beak, ending up with his "scree-kaw" cry. At times he seemed very aloof until I found a way to melt him—scratch his head. For that he would stand perfectly still while I sank my fingers into his downy feathers and rubbed his scalp. After I finished one side, he would turn around and have me do the other, meanwhile fluttering his eyelids in owlish bliss.

When the time came for him to leave, I took him to a distant hemlock grove where there were plenty of white-footed mice. There I perched him on a limb and stepped back a few feet to take his picture. Against the green branches, a perfect setting for his milk-chocolate-colored feathers, Coco already seemed to have lost his identity; he was no longer the little owl that had skimmed around my kitchen but some wild creature out of the north. He stayed on the limb, staring in my direction, so I walked over with my hand outstretched to give him a farewell pat. For a split second I thought I saw a friendly flicker in his yellow eyes. Then the shutter dropped, and I was looking at a stranger who turned his head and glided off into the woods.

3 〜

## ROBINS AND OTHER ORPHANS

*Eeny, Meeny, Miney, Moe*

# 3. Robins and Other Orphans

IT was soon after my adventure with the four little owls that I joined the Audubon Society and became one of their volunteers caring for injured wild birds. Since then I have bound the wounds of several hundred, been saddened by their suffering and gladdened by their recovery, and angered, too, at their senseless destruction through indifference and lack of understanding.

On the other hand, I am often gratified by the kindness of people who find helpless birds and the trouble they go to in order to aid them. One woman drove seventy-five miles to bring a convalescing sparrow to my small-scale shelter; she had been caring for the bird herself until she was called out of town. A few years ago I wrote a piece for an international magazine about a phase of this bird-saving work. A month later, via the publisher, I received an air-mail letter from Sweden. The writer had read my article and was puzzled about what to feed an injured swallow. I hurriedly dispatched the best diet I knew for a bird that lives almost entirely on winged insects: scraped lean beef, unflavored gelatin, and dried flies. Back came her grateful reply: the bird had thrived on the diet and eventually recovered.

## BIRD AMBULANCE

Of course not every one has been a success story. Sometimes people bring me fledglings that they have tried to raise but that, because of improper food and care, are too weak to survive. Sometimes birds arrive so badly injured they can never recover. In this case the only humane thing is to end their pain as soon as possible. Much as I dislike doing it, I saturate a piece of cotton with liquid chloroform and hold it firmly across the bird's nostrils; in seconds its eyes close. Then I put the limp body in a box, close the lid, and wait until the fumes finish the job. I hope it is painless; at any rate it is mercifully quick.

Only one thing I refuse to do, and that is to hatch eggs. At least once or twice every summer some child brings me a bird's egg it has found, hopefully expecting me to do something about it. A teacher even sent a youngster around with a nest that had fallen in the school yard to see if I could save the unborn robins.

My records show that little robins get in trouble more often than any other birds—or perhaps there are just more of them in the suburbs. If baby birds fall out of their nests, the best thing is to put them back; if they are old enough to hop or flutter, it is a good idea to perch them in a bush or tree out of harm. But when nests are destroyed, very young birds may need help to survive.

This was the case with three baby robins one spring. A housewife in my area found them after a bad storm near the pieces of their sodden nest, with no parent birds to protect them. She called the local animal shelter, which was unable to care for the birds but suggested that she contact Audubon headquarters. There she was given my telephone number, and later, over the phone, I made arrangements to pick up the robins. (Sometimes, when they learn my address, people bring the birds to me themselves.)

At home I put the three orphans in a small berry box lined with grass and tissues. This lining was to give the young birds' feet something to push against. If they had been placed on a hard, flat surface, their legs might have "spraddled." Because young birds

28

grow so fast, their legs could have set in a spraddled position and they might never have been able to walk properly.

There were only a few stiff quills of rolled-up feathers on their nearly naked backs, so I covered the birds with a bit of woolen cloth and kept them out of drafts. Baby birds must be kept warm at all times, since they are used to being hovered by their mother.

Soon they were thriving on their new nestling formula of chopped beef, grated hard-boiled egg, dried baby cereal, and powdered eggshell, plus wheat germ and vitamins. However, a worm from the garden set them chirping with joy and stretching their necks out for it. These worms supplied the live food that hand-raised passerines—small perching birds, including most songbirds—should have during their first week of life. One ornithologist uses bee larvae as the live food for nestling wild birds. With no access to a hive, I feed mine small earthworms or squishy caterpillars to make up their quota of live food. Although meal worms are good for older fledglings and adults, their tough skin makes them indigestible for very young birds.

At times I have been caught without the proper ingredients to make up the food mixture for an unexpected accident victim and have had to make do with what I have had in the house. For newly arrived patients, whether nestlings or adults, the critical thing is a quick meal, as most birds that come in are usually suffering, among other things, from lack of food. With this in mind I keep on hand a jar of strained baby beef, which I feed to young songbirds as well as injured adults. Mashed banana, bits of peeled cherries or grapes, and cut-up blueberries are also good as a quick snack. Another emergency food is well-soaked pellets of Gaines dog meal or canned dog food. This is excellent for crows, jays, starlings, and many shore birds, including ducks.

A pickup for very weak birds is a bird custard, made from one beaten raw egg and one-third cup of water (no milk). This is

29

baked like a regular custard and a small amount fed to the enfeebled patient every twenty minutes over a period of several hours. Beaten raw egg and cod-liver oil is often given to very weak birds with good results, but when they dribble it on their feathers and it hardens, they are a mess for a long time.

None of these emergency foods is a completely balanced diet; the nestling mixture is the best that I have found for young birds, even the young of seed eaters, whose parents feed them on insects and soft foods during the first weeks of their lives.

Although the three little robins in their berry box needed no water, they had to have a good deal of food in small doses. With a pair of blunt tweezers, I hand-fed them every half hour during the day. If I wanted an afternoon off, I had to get a bird-sitter. Babylike, they slept a lot, but, as I watched them one morning, they started to stretch and flap their wings. Soon they were preening themselves, which helped peel off their quill casings, those transparent sheaths which split and let the feathers expand into their final form. A week later, playing follow-the-leader, they hopped gaily out of their berry box and were promoted to a cage with a perch.

That was the day a friend brought me a young bluejay he had saved from a cat. Unhurt, but still shocked by its experience, it was mute and motionless. At feeding time, I lined the robins up on their perch, putting the scared newcomer at the end. Facetiously I began to count off, moving down the row with a tweezerful of food: "Eeny, meeny, miney—"

"Mo!" suddenly said the jay. Astounded, I picked him up. "Mo!" he repeated, fluttering his wings. "Mo! Mo! Mo!"

Then I realized that, though somewhat unusual for a bluejay, this was his special baby call—in fact his only note until he was old enough to jabber in true jay language. Naturally I named him Moe. And for days afterwards, the "eeny-meeny-miney" routine, with Moe calling out his name, delighted small-fry visitors.

The four birds were just learning to fly when a young kingbird was brought in. This insect eater had been found by some neighborhood children, who had tried unsuccessfully to feed him birdseed. Two days without food had turned him into a rather dispirited specimen of his spunky family, the tyrant flycatchers, so named because they will rout any bird encroaching on their territory, even an eagle. Soon, however, after a few hearty meals, this 7-inch bundle of black-and-white fury was boss of the kitchen. Although he was smaller than the others, none dared come within striking distance of his sharp bill. Once when they were both perched on the sill, Moe accidentally brushed him with a wing. That did it! The peppery little tyrant pounded Moe on the back, then began yanking at his tail. Alarmed, Moe flew off, but the King followed. Around the room they went, Moe shrieking and the King snapping at him. At last Moe ducked into the pantry and hid behind some jars while the King flounced back to the sill.

A week or so later, as soon as they could fly well, I released the five birds. If I had held them longer, they might never have learned to hunt for food; besides, it is against New York State law to harbor wild birds that can care for themselves. The hot-tempered King at once chased Moe and the robins away and settled down to his kingdom, the trees in the yard. The dogwood became his throne, and woe to any bird that even flew near it.

Strangely enough, he liked people. The very afternoon I freed him, he bounced down on my head with a friendly "Zeep, zeep." Flattered, I gave him a morsel of his favorite chopped beef, then he zoomed back to his tree. After that, at least once a day, he dropped down for a bit of food and gossip. Sometimes, not seeing him around, I would call or click a spoon against a dish. For some distant spot he would come winging through the trees with excited cries, as though saying, "Want me? I'm here!" If I were away, he often went to the next yard and chatted with my neighbor.

## BIRD AMBULANCE

One day a friend from a few blocks away drove up with the King in her car. She told me she had found her youngsters giving him a ride in their wagon. Although they were enjoying their feathered playmate, she was afraid he was injured until I explained he was a tame wild bird.

Weeks went by and the King stayed on, hunting moths, flies, and caterpillars in my garden. Toward the end of August, when his clan usually leaves for Central America to spend the winter, I grew worried about his lingering and laid it to the daily hand-outs I gave him. The last day of the month, after his usual snack, I set him in the dogwood tree. Next morning I missed him, and although I whistled, called, and clicked my spoon, I never heard his cheerful "Zeep, zeep" again. Evidently the age-old instinct of migration had won out over his fondness for hamburger.

A timberdoodle, better known as a woodcock, is a rare sight on the sidewalks of midtown New York. Yet on a spring dawn one of these odd birds was found on the steps of the Museum of Modern Art on 52nd Street and eventually became my patient. Flying north over the city, the woodcock had probably crashed into a tall building, for blood was oozing from a cut on its head. Seeing the bird on the steps, a truck driver picked it up, and since it was too early to get help for it, brought it to Long Island with him. Later, after calling Audubon headquarters, he got in touch with me. At home I smeared its head with ointment, then offered it moistened dog food, which it wouldn't touch. But when I dug some worms, it slurped them down like spaghetti; in the wild, woodcocks are believed to eat twice their weight in worms a day.

The next morning the account of the woodcock's accident appeared in the newspapers. One headline read: BIRD DISABLED BY SKYSCRAPER. In his story, a reporter called the bird "Woody," referring to it as a male, so I did too. However, since male and female woodcocks look alike, its sex was really unknown.

32

Short-necked and bobtailed, Woody was a chunky bird about the size of a pigeon. Against the dead leaves in his cage, his velvety brown and tan feathers were almost invisible, for no bird has better protective coloring. Like most night feeders, he had oversized eyes high on his head, the best place for them to be when searching for worms with his bill up to its hilt in mud.

His extra-long bill was unique. Instead of having the usual horny surface, it was encased in a thin, soft skin which covered a series of pits with highly specialized sense organs. When feeding in a bog, he could tell by pushing his bill into the ground what was there and where it was. Cordlike muscles running down the length of the upper bill permited him to bend the tip up or down to grip his food.

Handled gently, Woody soon got used to me, but for a wild bird he was very finicky about his four daily meals. He would eat only on a table, taking his fifteen muddy worms from a paper plate. When he had finished eating, he swished the dirt from his 3-inch bill in a dish of water, then fell into a blissful after-dinner reverie. I tried to break him of this habit by putting his worms in the cage. However, he stubbornly refused to pick them up and stalked off to a corner while the worms wriggled through the large-meshed netting.

Believing he was impatient to get to his breeding grounds, I released Woody as soon as his injury had healed. Besides, sixty worms a day meant a lot of digging. The day I freed him in a near-by swamp, he "froze" on a log in true woodcock fashion. Then with a whistling sound of his rounded wings, he took off, heading north-east toward the shore of Connecticut.

There, if everything went well, he may have courted a mate with the ancient woodcock ballet, first strutting like a rooster before raising and spreading his white-bottomed tail. Trailing his wings and throwing his head back, he would lay his bill against his chest. A few quick steps would follow, then a body contortion, and a burst

33

of loud "peenks." Spiraling straight up, he whistled a medley of clear notes before diving down and returning to his take-off point near the lady of his choice. After several encores, they probably flew off together toward some muddy bog and set up housekeeping, Woody's collision with that New York skyscraper completely wiped from his timberdoodling memory.

Another bewildered migrant was a female ruffed grouse brought to me by a policeman one October day. She had been found in a busy traffic center, madly dashing around for cover. September to November is the so-called crazy season for these birds, when one occasionally flies against a house or through a window; at this season they are found in the most unlikely places.

My patient looked something like a red-brown chicken with a fan-shaped tail that had a black band near the end. Unlike the male of her species that struts with wings lowered and ruffs raised high around his neck, her ruffs were inconspicuous. In captivity she seemed as tame as a pet hen, letting me stroke her feathers or pick her up. Fed on cracked corn and oats, she was staying with me until the week-end when I intended to take her to a bird sanctuary.

Meanwhile, because even my largest cage seemed small for her, I thought she would welcome some exercise. So, putting a long string on one of her legs, I began walking her in the garden. One whiff of the air of freedom had her racing around the yard, trying to get away. As she made a dash for the street, I grabbed her but caught only a handful of feathers. Somehow I was able to reel her in by the string. Then suddenly taking off like a kite on the end of the string, she flew onto the garage roof. I waited and waited for her to come down, but she decided to sit it out, and I was afraid I would break her leg if I jerked her down. At last I had to call a neighbor who got a ladder and prodded her into my waiting arms. A grouse does not lead well on a leash!

For a crippled or exhausted bird, however, exercise is out of the question. In fact, adult birds sometimes go into shock and literally die of fright if they are not kept quiet after being injured. In examining a small bird, I find it easiest to put my left hand around its back and wings, using slow, decisive movements. This prevents the bird from trying to flutter and agitate itself more; then with my right hand I part its feathers to look for wounds. Although at times a broken wing or leg may have to be set, a number of injuries heal by themselves if the bird is given proper food and rest.

A fair-sized cardboard carton holding food, water, and a perching stick makes a good temporary home. Covered with removable netting or screening and lined with papers or leaves, the box can easily be kept clean. In an ordinary birdcage, on the other hand, a wild bird may beat itself against the wires in an effort to escape.

Warmth is often a miracle worker in restoring exhausted birds, and the small brooder that I now have has worked wonders with adult as well as baby birds. Before I had this I often used a heating pad or a light bulb.

If there is much bleeding, I bathe the wound in ice water; warm water may cause hemorrhaging. Then I apply an antibiotic salve such as Myciguent, but never a carbolic antiseptic which might harm a bird.

Baby birds are not usually afraid and readily open their mouths for food. They should be fed every half-hour for a twelve-hour day by putting small bits into their mouths. When they have had enough, they refuse to swallow. A good rule is to wait until a bird has swallowed the previous morsel before putting any more food into its throat. And, of course, no seed for baby birds; they cannot digest it, even though their parents are seed eaters. Later when the birds are able to perch, their feeding time may be stretched to once every hour until they learn to feed themselves, always a happy day for a foster parent. One way to hasten this is to sprinkle their food with a little black loam from the garden.

35

## BIRD AMBULANCE

Most birds instinctively crave this black dirt, which scientists now find has organisms that destroy germs harmful to birds, particularly those causing intestinal inflammation. When the birds start pecking at the dirt, they inevitably pick up some food along with it and soon they are feeding themselves.

Over the years, I have learned not to give a baby bird water or milk from a medicine dropper. They do not need any liquid while they are in the nest, and if it is given forcibly, it may kill them. When they are old enough to perch, I offer them water in a shallow dish.

It is always wise to handle young birds and injured adults as gently as possible, and they often sense that you want to help them. It is kindness, too, to release them as soon as they can fly well and take care of themselves. Watching a former patient soar into the air is the best reward for helping a bird.

# 4 ～
## WAIFS WITHOUT FEATHERS

*Skippy*

# 4. Waifs Without Feathers

ONCE you become known as a person who takes care of baby birds, you are likely to be asked to take on other waifs of the animal kingdom—baby squirrels, baby bats, and even baby insects.

One June day a nurseryman with whom I do business came to my door with a cocoonlike object attached to a sprig of evergreen. Handing it to me, he explained, "A client had me cut down his yew hedge and I found this praying mantis nest in it. Maybe you could attach it to one of your bushes until it hatches."

"Well, yes," I said, a little bewildered but willing to try to save some of these insect-eating insects that have often been called the gardener's friend. "I'll see what I can do."

Afterward I wired to one of my own yews the twig with the 2-inch cocoon, noting its three bands, of which the middle one is made of little plates or scales, arranged in pairs and overlapping like the shingles on a roof. The edges of these are free, forming two rows of slits through which the young mantis escapes at the moment of hatching. The eggs are arranged in layers with the ends where the heads lie pointed toward the exits. One half of the new-hatched babies go out the right-hand door and the other half through the left-hand. When the mantis first makes her nest, she covers this belt of exit doors with a special white chalky material that contrasts with the dirty white color of the nest itself. The frosting-like decoration soon crumbles and falls off, exposing the doorway with its two rows of plates.

In time past the mantis and its nest were regarded with awe, and many superstitions grew up around it. Even now in parts of Europe the nest is believed to cure chilblains if it is squeezed and the affected part rubbed with the juice that oozes out. French farmers' wives still consider the nest a cure for toothache, calling it a *tigno*. They gather it under a certain phase of the moon and tuck it carefully in their cupboards against the day they may need it.

The mother mantis makes this extraordinary nest at the same time she lays her eggs. Producing from her body a sticky· substance, she mixes it with the air by whipping it into a froth. At first this foam is sticky but in two minutes it turns solid. In this sea of foam the mantis lays her eggs in layers, and as each layer is laid, it is covered with the froth, which soon hardens. As soon as the mantis has finished her egg laying, she leaves and never returns to see what becomes of her family.

Every day I examined the nest attached to my yew. Then one July morning action started. Fascinated, I watched dozens of blunt, transparent lumps swarming out of the middle slit. The baby grubs were reddish-yellow with thick swollen heads. Under the outer skin I could see their large black eyes, their mouths flattened against their chests, and their legs plastered to their bodies. At the moment of hatching, the youngsters wore a kind of skin coverall which let them move more easily through the winding passages in the cocoon. These paths would have been too narrow for their full-spread limbs to navigate.

With a magnifying glass, I could see this outer skin burst open near the chest, then the grubs wriggled and bent in a wild effort to tear off their little jumpsuits. Finally they freed their long slender legs and antennae and quickly climbed out on a cluster of yew needles.

When newly born, the babies were tiny replicas of their slender 3-inch parents, whose green coloring and gauzy wings make them quite attractive. Although mantises feed only on live creatures and are fierce as tigers in capturing their prey, they look harmless enough. Unique among insects, they have flexible necks, a feature which lets them turn their heads in all directions. In fact they almost seem to have faces. To the ancient Greeks, the mantis's slim, erect body and forelegs raised to the sky suggested a priest at prayer, and from this posture came the name praying mantis. Yet they are anything but angelic. I recalled that the adult mantis is cannibalistic but I had no idea at what age this trait appeared.

Sympathetic with their motherless plight, I reasoned they must be ravenously hungry, since they were so transparent I could see through them. With a blade of grass I carried one to my chrysanthemum bushes which, at that time of the summer, were covered with a type of plant lice called black aphids. Not yet five minutes old, the quarter-inch baby snatched an aphid in its tiny claws and began its first meal.

Back at the nest I hurried another mantis over and put it on the next plant. Soon I had a dozen bushes equipped with individual aphid eaters. Then I saw one bush without one. What I didn't see was a baby mantis on the underside of one of the leaves. When I put a second baby on that bush, the first one dashed out, grabbed its brother or sister with its claws, and bit off its head. The helpless victim shivered and raised its forearms in a gesture of supplication, a convulsive reflex no doubt. However, its ferocious killer showed no pity and went about the business of swallowing its kin.

Although I realized such things happen all the time, especially in the insect world, the incident depressed me. Remorsefully I went indoors, feeling like an accomplice to a murder.

Skippy was a gray squirrel with an unusual problem—he needed dentures. Before he was a month old (his age estimated by the fact that his eyes were still unopened) he had crawled out of his nest in a neighboring oak, lost his grip on a tree-top limb, and crashed to the ground. The surmise was that his mother had met with some tragic accident while away foraging for food and had been unable to return to her nursing babies. Except when desperately hungry, young squirrels seldom leave their cozy nests until at least thirty days after birth. By then their eyes are usually open and they can climb warily from one branch to another.

Appalled at the blood gushing from the baby squirrel's nose and mouth, his rescuer, who had heard the commotion and picked him up, rushed him to me in her clothes basket. The ice-water compress I applied finally stopped the bleeding, but my patient had a badly swollen mouth and the loss of his upper front teeth.

At first his puffed-up lips prevented him from sucking a bottle. Instead I fed him the customary formula for small mammals (one part evaporated milk to two parts warm water fortified with baby vitamins) from a medicine dropper. It was a slow process, but he showed his enthusiam by turning his battered little muzzle toward me and squealing eagerly for more. When the swelling had gone down a bit, I gave him his first meal from a doll's bottle. Lying on his back, he wrapped his paws around its neck and supporting the bottom with his hind legs, took a hearty swig and grunted contentedly. This was more like it!

By then his dark-brown eyes were fully open and button-bright, but, like most squirrels I have known, he was slightly myopic, depending on his keen nose to sniff out food.

His first solid meal was bread soaked in his milk which he sucked and nibbled at in spite of the absence of his two long uppers. A peeled grape too was soft enough to give the spice of variety to his nursery-type diet. The time came, however, when nuts should have become his major food. Here the loss of his teeth was a real misfortune. Even though I shelled peanuts and walnuts for him, he could not manage their hard kernels. Peanut butter spread on a slice of soft bread was the next best thing. The only drawback was that it got stuck in his fur and kept him forever grooming himself. The solution was small sandwiches; the bread outside kept his paws clean while the peanut butter supplied the protein he needed. I made a supply of these and put them in the refrigerator, passing them out when he seemed hungry. On these, plus the grapes, a slightly moistened cookie, and once a week a dab of vanilla ice cream laced with vitamins, he grew into a handsome squirrel with a fine bushy tail and appealing ways.

Since his eyes had been closed when I got him, he had never seen another squirrel. His first imprint was a human, and to him people were his kin. He rushed to greet all visitors, capering around their feet and, with the least bit of encouragement, climbing into their laps. Because of his deficiency, few people were afraid of him, since he could not bite, a tendency that even the tamest squirrels have as they get older. Children enjoyed holding him; he had a habit of putting one front paw on their chests and leaning back to peer into their faces as though searching for some one he knew.

Ever since his arrival, he had slept at night and sometimes napped during the day in his green sleeping bag, which was really an old woolen sock that hung in the corner of his cage. In the morning I opened his door, and while I had my coffee he joined me with his breakfast sandwich, sitting nearby on a stool. Then, as I got up to wash the dishes, he liked to start his climbing practice— on my bare legs. His needle-sharp claws were ideal for clinging to rough tree bark, and lacking that, he dug them vigorously into my ankles and hitched toward my knees. After a couple of such climbing bouts, and before I could shake him off, my legs had a network of canal-like ditches that were anything but sightly.

*43*

## BIRD AMBULANCE

Liking people, he wanted companionship and scampered gaily around me whenever I came into the kitchen. A paper bag was good for a wonderful game of hide-and-seek; he would crawl into it, peek out at me, then pull it over his head and wait for me to uncover him. Although the rest of the house was out of bounds, the kitchen and the so-called study where I keep my typewriter were enough of a playground for a small squirrel. After arranging the venetian blind to give myself the best light, I would start my typing. Then, click! the room would be darkened. Skippy had learned to manipulate the venetian-blind cord and kept me jumping up to adjust it all over again. It was worth the spank I gave him just to get my attention.

One day his tricks with the blind got to be too much, so I decided to banish him. As I picked him up, I cupped his face in my hand and told him what I thought of his antics. He cringed and whimpered as if his mouth was hurting. This led me to investigate, and I saw that his lower grinders had grown exceedingly long and were actually piercing his gums where his upper teeth were missing. My veterinarian suggested that I bring him in for a tooth treatment, which consisted of snipping those long lowers down to normal size again. He explained that, like all rodents, Skippy would have normally kept his lower teeth at their correct length by grinding them against his uppers when opening nuts and gnawing bark. Because of his accident this was impossible, and the lower teeth had kept on growing and might eventually have pierced his brain.

After his dental session, Skippy was his cheerful, inquisitive self again, pushing and prying into cracks and corners with his nimble little paws. It was near the end of summer and most of the birds had been released, so I put Skippy out in the shelter during the day, believing the fresh air and direct sun would be good for him. Clean-up day in that little room was the time when I picked up the newspapers from the floor, swept up crumbs and seeds, and carried the trash out in a basket. With my hands full, I closed the door with my foot. I was back in less than two minutes but the door stood partly open and Skippy was gone. I combed the nearby shrubbery first, then widened my search to the rest of the garden and later to the entire block. Calling and whistling, I expected any second to see his little furry body skittering toward me. But he never came.

The local newspaper printed the account of his disappearance, and the neighborhood children who had known and played with him took up the hunt. I emphasized his need for soft food, and they were as concerned as I was. "Maybe he'll find some berries to live on," one worried youngster suggested hopefully. "Maybe," I agreed, to make her feel better. But without his monthly tooth trim, Skippy's chances of survival were very, very poor.

Long before Batman became a national hero, fate tossed Bat Boy into my lap.

One July morning a frantic call brought me crashing into my neighbor's yard. "A bird or something's drowning," she cried excitedly, pointing toward her swimming pool.

Grabbing at a pair of thrashing wings, I lifted out a dark body. Holding it, I stood dumfounded at my first close-up of a mother bat with a baby clinging to her breast. The terrified mother struggled for a moment, then wrenched herself free and flew off, leaving her 2-inch baby in my hand.

In amazement I stared at the webbed wings and the fur-covered body ending in a flap of membrane that made a sort of tri-angular tail. Big ears jutted from a little head with the face of a scowling monkey. Feeling the warmth of my hand, the youngster cuddled down and began nuzzling my palm. "Hello, Bat Boy," I said, guessing at his sex, and adopted him on the spot.

At home I dried his wet fur with a cloth. Slowly he turned his head from side to side to watch me, meanwhile waving his extraordinary hands that had evolved into wings. Millions of years

45

ago skin formed between the fingers and arms of his ancestors, making them the only flying mammals on earth. As Bat Boy moved his arms, those layers of fleshless skin opened and closed like the cloth of an umbrella.

I let him investigate my hand. Propelling himself by his thumb, which was free and hooked for hanging, he made a grand tour of my palm, sniffing each finger like a friendly pup. Finally he crawled into my lap where he rested a while, then grasping my skirt, he flopped over my knee and, head down, fell asleep.

Afterwards I put him in a strawberry box, as I do with baby birds, and covered his back with a scrap of cloth. This didn't suit Bat Boy at all. In a second he flipped off his blanket and climbed out of the box. Then putting his unbelievably delicate feet on its edge, he swung over the side. There he settled himself comfortably, upside down as usual.

The curator of the Bronx Zoo identified my foundling as a *Myotis lucifugus,* or little brown bat. A common species in this country, these bats often roost in caves or trees as well as in abandoned buildings. The obliging curator also gave me a bat formula: one part evaporated milk in two parts of water, the same used for many other small mammals.

But how to give it to him? Even the tiniest doll's bottle was too large for his little bat's mouth. Hanging upside down from the side of the box, Bat Boy solved the problem by lapping it like a kitten from a demitasse spoon.

Like all babies, he slept a lot the first days I had him. Then one unhappy day he vanished. Certain that he couldn't fly yet, I searched the floor and even poked behind the stove trying to find his furry little body. At last I gave up. Hours later I discovered him in the pantry, hanging from the edge of the shelf paper. After that, although I put him safely in his box at night, I always found him in the same position on the closet shelf in the morning.

In a few days he was taking solid food—a mishmash of egg yolk, bananas, and meal worms—and growing fast. How fast, I learned one afternoon when I stepped into the kitchen. Raising his head, he fixed me with his beady eyes as though wanting me to pay attention. Suddenly he let go of his shelf hangar and launched into the air. Again and again he circled the room, wheeling and cutting capers close to the ceiling. He acted as if he wanted to be sure I was watching and being impressed with his flying skill. "Bat Boy," I laughed, waggling my finger at him, "You must have been practicing in secret."

As his forebears had done for more than fifty million years, Bat Boy flew by ear like a radar-equipped craft, sending out squeaks too faint for human ears. In this way, without using his eyes, he could breeze around outdoors at night, hunting insects. Indoors, beeping about two hundred times a minute, he flew in easy circles, avoiding obstacles by the echo that bounced back to him from them.

The first hint that sound guides bats came from an eighteenth-century experimenter who learned that blind bats performed normally but deaf ones couldn't find their way about. Later biologists belittled this theory, believing bats used some sixth sense or had a highly developed sense of touch. The role of their ears was not understood because it was assumed that there was nothing for bats to hear. But in 1939 at Harvard, Donald R. Griffin, now Director of the Institute of Animal Behavior of the New York Zoological Society, performed an experiment. By using electronic equipment, he showed that bats give out short, ultrasonic cries and guide themselves by the echoes, a process called echo-location. This is how man-made echo sounders detect submarines, but the bat's sonar is more delicately tuned.

One of the amazing things about bat echo-location is the speed with which the sounds are sorted out in the tiny brains of these remarkable creatures. They can distinguish the echo bouncing off tiny insects from the louder echoes coming from other objects.

## BIRD AMBULANCE

Much of their insect hunting is done in wooded areas where leaves and branches return stronger echoes than their insect prey. Bat watchers have made experiments proving that bats can dodge fine wires even when loud jamming noises blanket the frequency of their orientation sounds. These jamming experiments seemed to contradict what radar engineers call the "signal detection theory." In other words, blithely ignoring this engineering jargon, the bats heard echoes far below the level of any jamming noise and knew how to act on them at once. The brain of my little brown bat was less than one-thousandth the size of a human's. How did he come by this special talent?

Since Bat Boy's roost was in my kitchen, I had time to observe him as I worked. Ordinarily he slept much of the day. Awake, he often spent twenty minutes grooming himself. First he licked the fur on his stomach, then his leathery wings. Moistening his thumb, he rubbed it, cat-fashion, over his head and nose. Afterward he cleaned his ears by shaking his thumb inside. Next, holding on by one foot, he combed his fur with the other. An expert twister, he turned his body to smooth one side of his back, then changed his feet to finish the job. At last, tired out by so much activity, he would snooze again.

Once I offered him a moth that had crashed against the screen. Excitedly he reared up on his feet and wrists, then inched toward it like a cat stalking a bird. A quick pounce and it was in his mouth. But instead of eating it, he plopped down on his tail and curled its three-cornered flap in front of him. Dropping the moth in this pouch, he peered at it before swallowing it. Besides being a place to hold insects, this tail membrane also serves as a temporary cradle. Here the mother bat deposits her newborn baby and washes it before biting through the umbilical cord.

The neighbor in whose pool Bat Boy had almost drowned used to inquire about his progress, but she refused to come near him. "Too spooky," she always said. A very good friend canceled

*48*

her impending visit when she learned I had a bat in my house. Even the delivery boy, who used to come inside with packages, handed them in at the door and scooted off after he had once seen Bat Boy hanging from the kitchen shelf.

Most people feel this way about bats. Probably because they fly at night, they seem eerie and mysterious. Besides, legend has made them omens of bad luck that roost in haunted houses and hobnob with witches. However, in one country they are regarded highly. In the Chinese language the word for bat is *fu*, which is also the name of the character meaning happiness. In China the figure of a bat has come to stand for happiness or good luck and is often used in Chinese design. The picture of two bats on a gift means good wishes from the donor, and a popular charm in that country is a disk showing the tree of life surrounded by five bats with outspread wings. This talisman of the five bats is called *wu-fu* and denotes the five great joys of man: health, wealth, long life, good luck, and tranquillity.

For my part, I thoroughly enjoyed my interlude with Bat Boy. Since my earliest years I have been fascinated by wild creatures. When I was six I found a field mouse in the garage. Backing it into a corner, I caught it in a mason jar. For a few enchanted moments I stood transfixed while it twitched its whiskers and blinked. Then I made the mistake of handing it a piece of cheese. Naturally it bit me. I dropped the jar and the mouse quickly scurried away. Even though my thumb was sore for days, I still recall it as a delightful first experience with the world of nature.

Actually, bats are wonderful. Living in all parts of the world, they come in assorted sizes. The largest, the flying fox or Indian fruit bat, has a three-foot wingspread. The home of these giant bats is the tropical East where they live on fruit. Flying in large groups, they sleep by day and raid coconut plantations and mango groves at night. Suspending themselves head down, they roost in tall trees where they wrap their long wings around their bodies and doze during the day. It is reported that they sometimes sip the liquor from half-empty glasses left in Indian gardens after a party. This makes them tipsy. Returning home, they fall to the ground under their roosting tree and sleep off their hangover.

In contrast to these huge flying foxes, most bats have measurements in inches. Some feed on nectar and pollen by means of long snouts or brushlike tongues. One Central American species gaffs fish while flying over water. Many, like my little brown foundling, eat their weight in moths and mosquitoes every night. The majority of the 850 species are not only harmless but useful. The exception, the four-inch vampire of tropical America, nicks the skin of sleeping cattle with its razor-sharp teeth. Without waking its victims, it then sips their blood. People are also sometimes bitten.

As Bat Boy's furry body lengthened, his time in the air grew longer too. Although he still slept most of the morning, in late afternoon he made lively trips around the kitchen. One stunt he did again and again was to skim over and under the swinging rods of my towel rack without touching them. Apparently this is a kind of brinkmanship game bats like to play to test their echolocation ability. One naturalist tells of a pet bat that used to play tag with a whirring electric fan, deliberately flitting in and out of its spinning blades and always reappearing unhurt.

For almost a month Bat Boy lived with me. Then I felt that he could take care of himself, so one evening I took him to the door and opened it. I stroked his back for a moment while he reared up on his wrists, sniffing the warm air now fragrant with phlox and roses. Turning slowly, he gazed at me with what I fondly imagined was a farewell look. Then he flew up—but not out; instead he returned to the kitchen where he fluttered around his familiar pantry shelf. Suddenly, swooping over my head, he slipped out into the darkness.

I never saw Bat Boy again. But it did seem that the mosquitoes were not nearly so thick in my yard the rest of that summer.

# 5

## FRIENDLY FALCON

*Horus the hairdresser*

# 5. Friendly Falcon

VISITORS to the house one summer often got a surprising welcome in spite of my watchfulness. Coming inside, they would hear a whir of wings. Suddenly a brown bombshell would shoot out of the kitchen and land on their heads, clutching their hair with eight razor-sharp talons. In a most unladylike way, Horus, a female falcon, was saying hello.

Early that June, just as I was bringing in a bag of groceries from the car, I saw a policeman at my door. Startled, I wondered if I had passed a traffic light on the way home.

"I guess you'll know what to do with this," the husky six-footer said. With that he handed me a box punched with holes, adding, "I found this poor bird in the street and was afraid it would be run over."

Assuring him I would do what I could, I thanked him and he left. Then I hurried into the kitchen to examine the patient.

The newcomer was a young kestrel falcon, commonly called a sparrow hawk in this country. Her cinnamon-colored wings proved that she was a female, the male's wings being ash blue.

# BIRD AMBULANCE

Wisps of natal down still sprouted through the smooth feathers on her head, all that was left of her month-old baby dress. Although broad-shouldered and muscular, she had not yet reached her full length of 12 inches.

Blood oozed from her mouth, so I started to look for the cause. At that she threw herself on her back and slashed out with her talons, screaming wildly, "Kee! Kee! Kee!"

Speaking quietly while avoiding her claws, I told her I was sorry she had been hurt. That seemed to soothe her and she got up on her feet. "Kee-kee-kee," she began to wail softly, calming down and letting me sponge her pretty black-and-white face. Then I noticed at the base of her beak a nasty cut which I rubbed with salve. Barely able to fly, she had probably made a crash landing while trying out her wings.

Afterward I held out a strip of raw beef, but she backed away from my outstretched hand. I laid the beef across one of her claws, the approved way of getting birds of prey to eat in captivity. She shook it off and scuttled to a dark corner of the room. Finally I sat her on a stool, put the meat in front of her, and left.

When I looked in later, I was just in time to see her swallow the last scrap of beef and close one eye. Stepping into the room, I moved warily toward her. At once she sprang to life and jumped at me, catching her feet in my dress. Dumfounded, I let her claw her way to my shoulder. There she perched for a moment and, settling down, nestled her head against my cheek in the firm belief she had found a friend.

Horus had the long wings characteristic of true falcons. In fact she was the American variety of the Old World kestrel falcon, a pet since ancient times. Her diet in the wild was mostly grasshoppers and mice; "sparrow hawk" is a misnomer dating from colonial times. The hard-pressed settlers of our continent (with little time to study its wildlife) gave these birds the name of sparrow hawk, after a short-winged, yellow-eyed bird of prey found in Europe.

Although bird experts now frown on the name sparrow hawk for this little falcon, it still sticks.

Horus was a true aristocrat, with a pedigree going way, way back. I named her for the ancient bird-headed god of Egypt to whom her ancestors were sacred. Their mummified skins, found in the pyramids, show that the species has not changed in the last six thousand years. The sign of divinity in hieroglyphic writing, her image was carved on the throne of the pharaohs to symbolize their godlike power.

Horus slept in a big carton, but in the morning she jumped out and roamed around the kitchen. The best authorities on these birds say that falcons should never be kept in cages, since they may break their long flight feathers against the wires. Instead they should be put on a leash and given a stand. Horus never had a leash and her "stand" was wherever she decided to perch, a habit that had me following her around with newspapers.

Every bird of prey will try to reach the highest point in its immediate surroundings, and in the beginning when she could only make weak little flights, Horus worked out a way to get on the table: from the floor to a chair rung, then via the garbage can to the table. Later, after many failures, she managed to reach the curtain rod.

The first time she tried she walked to the edge of the table, bobbing her head, as though measuring the distance. Taking off, she nose-dived to the floor. I rushed over to see if she had been hurt, but she turned away, looking dazed and self-conscious. Then getting up, she pretended to study the design in the linoleum, as if to cover her embarrassment. But with a do-or-die spirit worthy of her noble breed, she kept at it. Often while working upstairs, I heard a thump that told me Horus had taken another belly-whopper. Then one afternoon I found her sitting proudly on the rod. "Bravo!" I applauded, as she graciously accepted my praise.

## BIRD AMBULANCE

From a perch on the windowsill, Horus could see into the garden. Here she preened for hours, pulling each pale breast feather through her beak, smoothing the red-brown plumage of her back, like a queen arranging her robes. Now and then she slowly raised her pointed wings, showing their striking undermarkings of cream and brown.

Those streamlined wings of hers make for lightning speed, the reason her Old World relatives were used to hunt small game before the advent of guns. For this sport, half-grown youngsters are taken from the nest or adults snared. After months of patient training, they are then outfitted with leash, bell, and a little hood which is put over the falcon's head to keep it from being frightened when traveling. This trick leads the bird to believe it is nighttime, and from it comes our word "hoodwink." Eyes covered in this manner, the picturesque hunter rides to the chase on the falconer's wrist. When the quarry is sighted, he slips off the hood and releases the bird.

In Europe, during the Middle Ages and later, the popularity of falconry and falcon keeping reached fantastic heights among the nobility. The nobles were devoted to their birds, lavishing money on their training and quarters (called mews). Elizabethan ladies were often so fond of their pet falcons that they could not bear to be separated from them and sometimes held them on their wrists at their wedding, preferring the beribboned bird to a bridal bouquet. However, falconry never became popular in America, and today it has all but died out except in the Middle East and India.

More than any other part of an animal, the eye seems to be the mirror of its intelligence. Looking at the eye of a bird, we see at once the brightness that reveals so well its vital, pulsing life. Typical of a falcon, Horus's eyes were outsized pools of melting brown. (If our eyes were in the same ratio to our bodies as a falcon's, they would be 3 inches across.) Alert, but gentle as a deer's, Horus's eyes at times seemed so expressive I could hardly bear it. Her vision also was capable of great flexibility; she could focus on objects far away or nearby—right at the tip of her beak for that matter—all in a moment of time; in fact, she could instantly transform her eye from a microscope to a telescope.

Once those keen eyes of hers had me running around in circles. Perched on the back of a kitchen chair, Horus started bobbing her head and staring into the dining room. That meant she had spied something. A mouse, maybe? I peered under the table and shook the draperies. Kneeling down, I followed her gaze to a spot on the floor. Almost twenty feet away from her an ant was carrying a crumb along the baseboard.

Watching bugs, dogs, and cars took up a good part of Horus's day. The rest was spent in games and flying practice. By the time she could fly well, her injury had healed. Very tame, even with strangers, she liked to sit on people's heads. Mine, where she could use her creative talents, was a favorite playground. Anchoring her talons in my braids, she pulled out loops of hair to give a scalloped, ringleted look. After that, she strutted around on top, eying the effect. More fluffiness over the ears? Too much now? Too little? We hairdressers have our problems. Then, tiring of her restyling job, she would yank out the hairpins and let my hair tumble down my back.

Another game of hers began one morning when I dropped an onion. From her windowsill perch, she watched it roll, then swooped to grasp it. This gave me an idea. I crumpled some paper into a ball and tossed it to her. She pounced on it, turned away, only to flash around and pat it with her claw like a kitten. Afterward, balancing on top of the paper ball, she started it spinning until she fell off. Then with surprising agility she would throw one leg out sideways and snatch at her make-believe prey with her flexible talons. At last she put an end to all the nonsense by holding the paper in a viselike grip and tearing it to bits. From then on, those paper balls were an exciting game for her, as well as preparation for her role of huntress.

But for a while there was no need for her to hunt; instead she lived on raw beef and cod-liver oil. Twice a week she was given a chicken head which she ate feathers and all. This supplied the roughage all birds of prey need to keep them healthy.

For over a month Horus had been queen of my kitchen. Then one evening a neighbor brought me a box containing a bird that had been nearly hit by a car. With womanly curiosity, Horus flew to my shoulder while I opened the box. Together we peered inside and saw—another sparrow hawk.

This newcomer, also a female, I judged to be about three weeks old, since there was still a good deal of baby fuzz on its head and shoulders. Although it could not fly yet, it did not seem injured. As I picked it up, it puffed itself into a ball and hissed at me. "Now you've got a playmate, Horus," I said, hoping the youngster would feel more at ease with her.

With hurt surprise, she watched me offer the little hawk a piece of *her* meat. Then she whirled and grabbed it away. She had already been fed, so I knew she was not hungry. But, absorbed with the other bird, I thought nothing about her inhospitable action.

To let them get better acquainted, I put the two birds near each other on the floor. Horus stepped back and glared at the intruder. Shrieking wildly, she blasted the youngster with unmistakable fury. A moment later, I thought she was having a fit. With head lowered and wings partly open, she began to stamp her feet. Every so often she jerked her tail and jumped into the air. Suddenly she lunged at the unwary newcomer with an outstretched claw, but I snatched the little hawk away and kept them apart until Horus was released. Afterward it dawned on me that Horus had been doing a sort of war dance, working herself into a frenzy before pitching into her rival.

By August Horus was full grown, with a wingspread of 23 inches. Her body was beautifully shaped and compact with no trace of that earlier fluffiness. The lines of her rounded head were clean-cut and precise, flowing over a short neckline into the broad shoulders, then tapering to her pointed wings. When alert, she sat upright, neck stretched and eyes almost bulging. Yet she moved her head slowly and deliberately without any of the jerky nervousness of a short-winged hawk.

She seemed quite content to stay with me, but I knew she would be better off leading the wild life for which she was meant. Yet parting from her was a wrench. Her habit of perching on people's heads made it risky to release her in a residential neighborhood; there was always the chance she might be recaptured. Instead I took her to a distant wildlife sanctuary.

In a sunny spot teeming with grasshoppers, which I hoped she would soon learn to catch, I set her on my wrist and waited for her to soar happily off. But she clung to my arm. For fully ten minutes, I walked up and down, telling her about the joys of freedom. "Kee-kee-kee?" she inquired doubtfully, as though she could not understand why I wanted her to go. Once she raised her beautiful wings and I thought she was ready, but she folded them and turned to me with such a sad look in her expressive eyes that I swallowed a lump in my throat.

At last I had to throw her into the air. Flying to a nearby tree, she perched on a dead branch. When I left, she was still sitting there forlornly. "She'll soon get used to the outdoor life," I told myself. And I believed she would. But I wondered about my falcon—would she miss her human friend?

Although the second falcon grew up to be a beautiful bird, she lacked Horus's personality. When released, she shed no tears.

# 6 ～

## BIRD IN A SLING

*Falcon in traction*

# 6. Bird in a Sling

In caring for wild birds, bone injuries are probably the worst to handle. The fracture of a wing in a small bird—below sparrow size—is the hardest to set, because human fingers are too clumsy to manipulate the tiny bones, and a splint or cast may do more harm than good. Unless the wing hangs at a very abnormal angle, I just confine the little cripple in a box without a perch, give it food and water, and hope for the best. If the bird is kept quiet, its bones knit so fast (usually in five days) that there is a good chance of its being able to use the wing again.

For wing fractures of robin-sized birds, I put the injured wing in a natural position on the bird's back, laying the end of the injured wing on top of the good wing for support and taping the wings together with adhesive where they cross near the tail. After a week, with luck, the wing is fully usable.

But larger birds—hawks, gulls, ducks, or geese—I rush to my very good neighborhood veterinarian, who not only has a unique understanding of birds but is an ardent bird watcher himself and a member of our local bird club. He usually X-rays the bone first and then, after giving the bird an anesthetic, sets it. After a specified time, I take the convalescent back to him to have him remove the cast and assess the amount of healing that has taken place.

A break in a bird's lower leg (metatarsus) is usually not too hard to set. The shank is put in a tube of stiff paper or a split quill feather, care being taken not to stop the circulation in the foot. Stroud advocates a foot sling to help keep the bones in alignment and prevent the bird from being crippled, and my experience bears this out. Although a quill or tube can hold the leg straight, it does not prevent the foot from getting twisted. The sling, made of soft string, is looped under the bird's foot and wound around its body, leaving the wings free for balance. In this way the bird can stand on one foot for the few days needed to heal the break.

I always thought that broken legs were easier to handle than broken wings until the day a male kestrel falcon was brought in with both thighs broken. In this case, a successful setting seemed impossible, for, in thrashing his body around, he continually disturbed the splints. Upon consultation, I was advised to destroy the bird.

But looking at him carefully, I was touched by the sculptured beauty of his noble head and sickle-shaped wings. Like those of Horus, my first falcon patient, his eyes were so expressive that I imagined he was pleading with me to spare his life. I felt I just had to try something.

For suggestions I turned to my husband who was always able to come up with a solution to my toughest bird problems. In his workshop, he put together a wooden frame, 10 inches long and 6 inches high, across which he tacked a piece of coarse cotton netting, making a sort of hammock. I clipped the feathers from the bird's thighs and splinted the broken bones with a lollipop stick, then wrapped them firmly with adhesive tape. Cutting two slits in the netting, I lowered the bird into it, one leg hanging through each slit and the feet just touching the bottom of the frame. To keep the bird from moving his legs and disturbing the splints, my husband made a small wooden block. I inserted this like a wedge between the bird's feet and taped it to them.

The ten days that the little falcon sat in his hammock would have been irksome to any human and to a free-flying bird they must have been doubly so. But he was a wonderful patient, never struggling to rid himself of his bonds and only occasionally raising his tail to keep his droppings from soiling his feathers. Of course I had to feed him by hand and hold his water dish when he drank.

When the time came to remove his splints, I began to worry. Suppose the authorities were right and no bird with two broken thighs would ever have any use of its legs. I fairly held my breath as, free of his bindings, I stood him on the floor, To my dismay, he toppled over, with his legs sprawled at a crazy angle. Had I prolonged the poor creature's suffering only to be obliged to end his life?

I examined the places where his thighs had been broken. Although the thighs were somewhat swollen, they seemed firmly knit. Taking heart, I recalled my own broken wrist and how weak it had been when the cast was taken off. It had been days before I had any use of it. It was days before the falcon could shuffle his mended legs, and for a while after that he walked stiffly, but eventually his legs grew strong and seemed as good as new.

One morning I took him to the same grasshopper-stocked field where I had released Horus the summer before. But his was no reluctant departure. When I opened the box, he sprang lightly out, ran a few steps, then took to the air. I watched until he was only a speck in the sky, his ordeal in the hammock forgotten. At times it pays to try the impossible.

Although many birds are grounded because of bone injuries, one that came to me needed an eye specialist. This patient was a black-and-white hairy woodpecker, a male, as shown by the red spot on the back of its head. Typical of these birds, it had a hard, pointed bill, an ideal tool for digging into bark. This chisel-like beak, backed by its large head with a thick skull to absorb the shocks of pounding, could be driven deep into the hardest wood.

These hairy woodpeckers live on Long Island all winter. In fact, a teacher had picked this one up from a pile of snow in a nearby schoolyard. After calling the Audubon Society, he brought the bird to me.

Although the woodpecker had no visible wounds when I examined him, I noticed his eyes were half shut and I thought he was sleepy. After giving him some food, I put him in a cage for the night. The next day I found his eyelids stuck together and the bird frantically scratching at them. With warm water and cotton, I managed to get them open. All the while I was bathing his eyes, he was very quiet and afterward seemed quite friendly. Hitching up my arm, he hooked his toes in my collar and clung to my shoulder like a corsage of feathers.

But the following morning he was again tearing at his encrusted eyes. Fearing he might blind himself with his sharp claws, I took him to the Bronx Zoo. Mr. Scott examined his inflamed lids under a strong light and rubbed some salve on them.

"Leave the bird here for a while," he advised. "He may need some more treatments."

Of course I agreed, and later, after his eyes had healed, the woodpecker was released in the zoological park. There, I learned, he stayed for several years, often probing for borers in the trees near the main birdhouse.

Scientists have definite ideas about why birds behave as they do. The gist of their theories is that wild birds are more or less feathered robots that respond to certain stimuli in a predictable way. Not looking at them with the same detachment as these behavior experts, I have found birds to be individuals with distinct personalities. In the course of time, I have met many different kinds—meek ones, scrappy ones, shy ones, and show-offs, but with the arrival of Kelly on St. Patrick's Day I acquired a clown.

A herring gull with a broken wing, Kelly was brought to me by a kind-hearted Irishman who had found him on a gale-swept beach. His rescuer had named him even before taking him to an animal hospital. There his wing was put in a cast, but the bird, whose black-tipped gray wings had a normal spread of almost 5 feet, was too big for the busy attendants to cope with during the necessary three weeks of convalescence, so his rescuer brought him to me.

Gulls are web-footed water birds that act as scavengers, patroling beaches and shores for refuse. They gather in flocks in harbors or wherever fish are thrown away, at canning factories or fish wharfs. Sometimes schools of fish are killed by disease or frost and are cast up by the tide. Gulls soon gather, and in a twinkling hundreds of smelly fish are gone. These birds flock where sewage is discharged and garbage dumped at sea. By ravenously gobbling down decaying vegetable and animal matter, they keep our coasts clean of refuse, doing the job of a corps of sanitation men.

Around farms near the coast, gulls sometimes follow the plow for grubs and worms. When locusts swarm, gulls often gather from miles to feast on them. In fact, gulls nesting on Great Salt Lake in Utah are credited with saving the first crops of the early Mormon settlers. As a plague of locusts ravaged the precious grain, huge flocks of gulls descended on the fields and devoured the insects. To commemorate this good deed, the Mormons in Salt Lake City have erected a lovely statue to the gulls.

Although a gull in the wild thrives on all sorts of garbage, in captivity it is very often a fussy eater, and even getting it to taste *anything* is an accomplishment. Overcome by his ordeal, at first Kelly refused to eat. Force-feeding one of these strong-billed birds takes patience, courage, and a complete disregard of pain, for it is apt to nip you on any unprotected part. After a long scuffle, I got Kelly to swallow one small piece of fish, but it left him queasy and the next moment he vomited it up. Remembering that shore birds often feed in the surf, I put some small pieces of fish in a pan of shallow water and left him caged in the basement. After he got over his fright, he began to eat by himself, happily dunking his fish bits up and down before swallowing them with evident relish.

At first I wondered whether a sea bird's drinking water should be salt. After several inquiries, I learned that it is not necessary to give a fish-eating bird salt water to drink in captivity, as there is enough salt in its sea-food diet. Although shore birds in the wild do drink salt water, a good deal of salt has to be eliminated by the kidneys or by salt glands behind the nostrils; only a small amount is needed for digestion.

Like most shore birds, Kelly loved to swim. Gulls are excellent swimmers, but although often seen on the water, they do not swim very far when they are able to fly; at this they are masters. They can fly forward, drift backward, or veer gracefully in any direction. In calm weather they flap along like herons, but when the wind blows they soar and wheel and are able to ride updrafts from the waves, from the sterns of vessels, and from dunes and cliffs. They often circle the water until they spot some floating object that looks like food, then pick it off the water in flight or drop down and swim to it.

To keep Kelly from taking a swim in his water dish and getting his wing cast wet, I had to put his drinking water in a narrow-necked jar. In spite of this, he tried hard to take a dip. Plunging his bill deep in the jar, he threw a beakful of water over his white head, then let it trickle down to his shoulders. Paddling like a steamboat, he shuffled around the floor of his cage, leaning sideways to become better "immersed." Then standing up after his swim, he shook imaginary moisture from his back and tail, as he carefully preened his breast.

Gulls are known to be playful birds, and Kelly was no exception. His first toy was a stick which he carried around in his bill, constantly picking it up and tossing it. One day I threw him a battered rubber ball. He squinted at it from all angles before touching it. Then holding it in his beak, he jumped up on the egg crate he used for a lookout perch and deliberately slammed it to the floor. Doubtless he mistook the ball for a clam and hoped to break it open by smashing it against something hard, as gulls have a habit of doing. When it rebounded and whacked him on the head, he let out a wild "Ki-ou." Then the novelty of a bouncing clam got to him. He dropped the ball again but this time caught it like a professional shortstop. After that he found the game such fun that he often played it, rarely missing a bounce.

In three weeks I removed his cast. The bone had knitted nicely, and as soon as his wing was strong again, I decided to let him go. A logical place to release him was that unique Wildlife Refuge in Jamaica Bay where travelers flying to and from Kennedy International Airport can look down on its marshy islands.

Less than twenty years ago this refuge was an eighteen-mile wasteland in the shadow of Manhattan's skyscrapers. But Herbert Johnson, its dedicated manager, has transformed the barren area into a green oasis for birds and nature lovers. He lives there now in a brown-shingled cottage, keeping an eye on plant and animal life. His boast is that he has the only bird sanctuary in the world with a subway running through it. Moreover, if aroused conservationists can halt the disastrous proposal to extend the airport runways into the refuge, it may remain the only place where feathered and human migrants co-exist. Fifty thousand visitors each year come to this sanctuary by car or by subway to the Broad Channel station.

But today, the Jamaica Bay sanctuary, like many other wildlife sanctuaries in America, is threatened by "progress." With air traffic on the increase, transportation officials are casting covetous

BIRD AMBULANCE

eyes on this piece of marshland close to Kennedy Airport. They want
to fill in the marshes and build more runways which would eventually destroy the refuge. Even if this new construction left a portion
intact, the need to eliminate the birds as a hazard to flight operations
would certainly follow.

Mention of airplanes makes Johnson look grim as he sur-
veys the teeming birdlife attracted to the area. Though old enough
to retire, he will not consider it, vowing, "I'll stay at this sanctuary
until I wake up some morning and find jets using the nature trails."
In the meantime, like many conservationists aroused by the destruction of our natural environment, he is pinning his hopes on the
counterproposal to put the area under federal protection.

Almost twenty years ago, Johnson, a long-time Park Department employee, started work on the project, using vegetation
that gives food and cover for birds as well as grasses to stop erosion.
Now it is a haven for more than three hundred kinds of wild birds
that use the many inlets of Jamaica Bay as well as the two ponds
created by the dredging operation for the subway. As these man-
made hollows collected rain and became almost fresh-water lakes,
aquatic plants such as widgeon grass, musk grass, and eelgrass took
root there. Soon afterward the birds arrived and have been coming
ever since. Ducks quickly discovered the sea lettuce at the bottom
of the ponds, and soon black skimmers and terns were nesting in the
beach grass.

By far the most spectacular birds are the American and
snowy egrets that once were nearly extinct. In summertime now
these graceful herons lay their eggs and raise their babies un-
molested in this refuge, astounding visitors with their breath-
taking beauty. The noisiest residents are the gulls—black-backed,
herring, and ring-billed—whose shrill cries are heard every season
of the year.

It was a great day for Kelly when I drove him to the
sanctuary. Riding on the back seat of the car in a covered box

topped with a brick, he heard his relatives' voices long before we reached the sanctuary. Excited by those familiar sounds and the smell of the salt marshes, he completely lost his head. Knocking off the brick and box cover, he scrambled toward the half-open car window. Too big to squeeze through, he climbed on my shoulders where, bracing his legs against my neck, he tried to straddle my head. With my hands on the wheel. I was in no position to wrestle with him, so I let him stay. Foiled in his attempt to escape, Kelly screamed his frustration at every passing car. As we approached some fishermen on a bridge, he poked his head out and blasted them in furious gull language.

"What the—?" one dumfounded man blurted, waving his rod in our direction.

My face was crimson but I kept my eyes on the road for the longest mile I have ever driven. When we finally arrived and I opened the door, Kelly rocketed from the car. Splashing down in a nearby cove, he immediately took his long-awaited bath, while I hurried home for a thorough shampoo.

# 7

## A HAWK LOST, A DUCK SAVED

*Duck in a tub*

# 7. A Hawk Lost, a Duck Saved

TRAGEDY sometimes follows comedy here at my bird shelter. When Red, a big red-tailed hawk, was first brought in, I reached for my heavy gauntlets, a shield against his talons. After one glance, I saw I wouldn't need them.

Although no wounds showed among the brown feathers of his back and his speckled breast was unscarred, he lay helpless on his stomach. All too obviously, his legs were paralyzed. Crumpled and still, the front inner claws and back claws felt lifeless. Normally these are the ones which exert the viselike pressure that kills so mercifully quick. The two outer claws that balance the foot were also limp.

A bird lover had found this hawk by the side of a lonely road on the north shore of Long Island and had taken him at once to an animal hospital. X rays showed no broken bones. It was the doctor's opinion that a nerve injury had caused the paralysis, the result, perhaps, of a sudden downward swoop against some wires. This sounded reasonable, since the hawk had been found near a crisscross of overhead cables. Massive doses of vitamin $B_{12}$ were prescribed and my nursing care was enlisted.

# BIRD AMBULANCE

My red-tail belonged to that subfamily of hawks known as *buteos,* the broad-winged mouse eaters, of which there are some twenty-five kinds in the world. These birds are medium- to large-sized raptors, with shorter legs and tails than those of the quick, dashing accipiters whose broad wings and long tails give them the speed and control of movement necessary to fly swiftly through the woods, to check their speed quickly, and to make the abrupt turns needed in their hunting. A typical accipiter is the pearly-breasted goshawk that was once used in falconry. In feudal days Japanese falconers used the goshawk to hunt cranes. No hunting goshawk was entitled to wear the royal purple jesses until it had killed the most noble of all game, the great Manchurian crane. Though this crane was twice the goshawk's size, it was no match for that fast-flying accipiter.

Preferring to soar lazily in wide circles, the red-tail glides gracefully down and drops on the branch of a dead tree or high post. There it spends hours, quietly waiting to pounce on mice, wood rats, or any small mammal or snake that will make a meal. In summer and fall, particularly in our western states, red-tails show up during a plague of locusts and gorge themselves on these pests. As their food habits show, these hawks eat mainly insects and rodents.

Though Red was too helpless to hurt even a fly, he still could not be allowed to convalesce in the screened shelter where three crippled robins and a one-winged dove are living out their lives. Although his food was rodents, he would have terrified them, for they instinctively regard anything with a hooked beak and talons as their enemy. Not so long ago, man did too and often shot some of our most useful birds. Even today, in spite of a mountain of evidence that hawks are beneficial, and the protection of state laws, some hunters and farmers destroy them, stubbornly refusing to recognize their worth. Sometimes the red-tail's habit of perching on a handy fence post may cost it its life. Its executioner is the vicious pole trap, a devilish contraption, outlawed but still used occasionally, that is put on posts and poles and catches the perching bird, breaks its leg, and holds it prisoner until it dies a slow and painful death.

Besides destroying many crop-eating rodents, hawks are an important link in nature's scheme, assigned to a specific role. Carnivores must kill to live, but few (with the exception of man himself) kill for the lust of blood-letting. When the hawk hunts, it is either a clean miss or an instantaneous kill for a meal. In nature the hawk's skill in hunting is balanced against the prey's ability to escape. In this way only the strong and healthy of either species survive. Realizing that birds of prey must hunt to live, I admire their beauty and spirit.

Even in the depths of woe, Red had spirit. Although he could barely raise his regal head, his yellow eyes looked boldly into mine; there was wildness in them but not fear. Gently I slid a folded towel under his breast. This propped him enough to let him swallow the much-needed food I offered.

"That bird must be starved, he's had nothing to eat for twenty-four hours," his rescuer had said as he left.

Red's appetite proved it. He ate five strips of raw beef before pausing to drink from the water bowl I held out to him. Again he turned his eyes toward mine, and though there was no softening of his gaze, I felt that unmistakable bond of understanding that sometimes springs up between animals and humans. Some scientists believe that if birds accept food from you, they trust you. Perhaps they think you are like a parent or mate offering a gift of food.

By covering a corner of my basement with newspapers and arranging some discarded window screens, I made an enclosure large enough for Red's comfort. Hopefully I added a heavy branch against the time he would be able to perch again. Every day I sprinkled his raw beef with vitamin concentrate. Every second day I scissored the feathered skin from the chicken heads donated by my butcher. This supplied the necessary "fur or feather" roughage Red needed.

Day after discouraging day I examined his feet. For a long time there was no sign of improvement. Then one morning I found him scrabbling around, trying to stand. Thereafter I rubbed his claws to help circulation, adding massage to my nursing care.

Although progress seemed maddeningly slow, the time came when I felt his grip on my finger. I supported him a little as he wobbled to his feet. Then, wings spread to their full 4-foot width and screaming like a triumphant eagle, he stepped up and perched proudly on my wrist. He turned his head all around, as if he was seeing his surroundings with new and masterful eyes. Then he stepped slowly down and fluffed and shook his feathers until they stood out in all directions. At last his long period of invalidism was over.

Soon he was able to eat in true hawk fashion, holding his meat between his claws while he tore off pieces with his beak. In a month his recovery was so nearly complete that I began to think of releasing him.

But time was running out for Red. One day he abruptly stopped eating, and his shrill scream dropped to a hoarse rattle. He drank a great deal of water, which is unusual for a healthy hawk. I bought some specially tender beef and tried to coax him to take it by offering him thin pieces in my fingers. In this way I got him to take a little nourishment but not for long. The day came when, turning his head dejectedly, he refused even the tiniest slivers. As he did so, I noticed a swelling at his throat and lost no time in getting him to my veterinarian.

"An impaction that an operation will take care of," he reassured me.

However, during the surgery, the doctor found a fast-growing tumor so embedded in the hawk's chest and larynx that it could not be successfully removed. Since Red was already under an anesthetic, he was given a little more to end his suffering. Of course, under the circumstances, it was the only thing to do, but I mourned my majestic hawk.

The night after I dismantled Red's pen I received a telephone call from Atlantic Beach. It was from a bird-banding cooperator, one of about a thousand doing this work in the United States and Canada under permits issued by the Fish and Wildlife Service. They trap birds in order to put metal bands on their legs bearing a number, date, and the address of the Fish and Wildlife Service and hope that where and when such a bird is found, it will be reported to the proper authorities.

My bird-banding acquaintance had found a sea duck, an oil-pollution casualty, and asked if he might bring it over. That was in March 1967, at the time when the *Torrey Canyon* disaster was making grim headlines. The 1000-foot tanker, en route from the Persian Gulf to Pembrokeshire, had foundered off the coast of Britain, spilling some hundred thousand tons of crude oil into the waters along the French and English coasts. Racing against time, the British tried to save their beaches by dissolving the advancing slick with detergents. But due to lack of experience, there was widespread misuse of these caustic chemicals; diluting instructions were ignored and the detergents were often used full strength. From the wildlife point of view, the use of detergents made the gobs of oil from the *Torrey Canyon* a double disaster. Thousands of migrating sea birds were caught in the blackened tides which eventually became their grave. Thousands more exhausted and dying birds, their feathers clotted with oil, were picked up on the beaches.

"The worst wildlife catastrophe on record," one horrified observer declared.

Ironically many waterfowl deaths were due to the caustic action of the detergents. Rescuers picked up birds with sores around their beaks where they had tried to preen their burning, itching

79

feathers. After they died, biologists found their livers were swollen from the effects of the cleansers.

Aroused by the pitiful plight of the survivors, a sympathetic public sent money, cleaning rags, and help. Bird shelters were set up along the shore. Volunteers came from everywhere. One hairdresser closed his shop to clean the oiled birds and dry them with his hair dryers, prisoners helped care for some, and a group of teen-agers converted their club into a bird hospital. However, people were warned against using strong soaps or cleaners to remove the crude oil, as these would also remove the natural plumage oil. In the case of water birds, this can be fatal, causing them to sink to the bottom and drown when they settle on the water. This loss of buoyance, known as "wet feather," often occurs when a bird becomes coated with oil and wrong methods are used to remove it.

If, in spite of all precautions, wet feather does occur, only a complete moult—a lengthy process lasting up to six months—will give the bird its natural waterproof covering again. Needless to say, cleaning the plumage of a badly oiled sea bird is risky business and not to be undertaken lightly. In addition, fright and physical exposure may cause the death of a rescued bird.

The British Broadcasting Company gave out the information for handling the oiled victims of the *Torrey Canyon,* and although the bird experts never quite agreed on the best method, Fuller's earth (a mixture of clay and fine siliceous material, sold in most drug stores), prepared chalk, lard, and salad oils were suggested for the job. Worked into a bird's oiled feathers, these break up the heavy clots, and, with luck and many baths in clear water, the plumage becomes normal.

Although my sea duck's plight was not caused by the *Torrey Canyon,* he benefited by the advice broadcast from the other side of the Atlantic. In his case some oil slick off our own shore had coated his dark feathers, all but obliterating his white eye ring and wing patch, the distinguishing marks of his species, the white-winged scoter.

After his daily rubdown with Fuller's earth to break up and wear away the clotted oil, I gave him a swim in my bathtub. He enjoyed this more than I did, because I had to scrub the oily ring he left. This became my yardstick of progress—as the ring grew fainter, I knew I was winning the battle against the oil.

Luckily he was not a fusssy eater and gobbled everything in sight *except* the special duck pellets I ordered for him. These he wouldn't touch. Eventually we settled on a mixture of dog food and chopped clams, sprinkled with cod-liver oil.

By May his feathers seemed perfectly normal, and as far as I could tell, the dreaded wet-feather condition had been averted. Now I let him stroll freely around the yard, where he lolled and preened contentedly, at times chasing after me for food. Although he often stood up and flapped his wings, he made no attempt to leave. I mentioned this to his rescuer when he phoned one day to ask about the bird.

"That duck knows he's got a good thing going," he joked. "It'll take a sniff of salt water to get him airborne."

The Jamaica Bay Wildlife Refuge seemed an ideal place to release my rehabilitated duck, since it has both fresh-water ponds and a salt-water inlet, giving him a choice. It was almost sunset when the duck and I arrived. All the while I was untying his box, he kept beating his wings with excitement. Once free, he raced with outstretched neck to the edge of the pond. There he paused a second before wading in. After paddling a short distance, he opened his wings and took to the air with noisy flaps. Higher and higher he mounted, circling the pond and inlet, then with a series of wild quacks, headed straight out to sea.

With mixed emotions I wished him "Happy landing," nagged by the report on the birds treated during the *Torrey Canyon* disaster. Although they seemed fully recovered and in good plumage, banding returns showed that a third of the survivors died soon after they were released, perhaps because they were too weakened by their ordeal to feed or rest on rough waters. In the case of my departed patient, I could only hope his luck would hold.

# 8

## THE WARBLER THAT CAME TO DINNER

*Dining in*

# 8. The Warbler That Came to Dinner

A REPORTER called him "The Bird That Came to Dinner and Stayed and Stayed." That newspaper caption was bigger than the mini-sized waif it described—a male pine warbler that had been buffeted by a wind storm. From beak to tail-tip he was only 5¼ inches and weighed 18 grams or 3/5 ounce.

After an autumn gale a Queens housewife found him in her shrubbery, one white-barred wing hanging low. Because of his green and yellow feathers, she thought he was an escaped canary and put him tenderly in a cage with seed and water.

But this bird's slender bill, designed for spearing little spiders and other soft insects, could not crack the hard seeds. Starved for lack of proper food, he finally collapsed on the bottom of his cage. His frantic rescuer telephoned several animal shelters, but none could tell her what to do. At last she called the local paper, which obligingly gave her my address. As a result, the little victim of the storm was rushed to my door in a taxi and the newspaper printed his story.

## BIRD AMBULANCE

Lying on his side in the cage, the bird was too feeble to peck at the egg and wheat germ I hurriedly mixed. In desperation I added water, making a thin gruel that I dribbled along the side of his bill. Miraculously he was able to swallow enough to give him strength to stagger to his feet. Then he spied the rest of the food and dragged himself to the dish. Egg spattered his breast, crumbs crusted his eyes, as his bill flew like a sewing machine needle to fill his empty stomach. At last, stuffed to bursting, he clung to the edge of the saucer and gazed at the leftovers. I had to pry him off to get him back in his cage.

Quiet and shy at first, after a few good meals he was quite at home. When I put fresh food in his dish, he hopped confidently on the back of my hand and cocked his head to watch. And when he curled his fragile claws around my finger and nibbled bits of chopped beef from my hand, I was absurdly touched. Although his wing was mending, I wondered if it would be strong enough to carry him to his winter home in Mexico. But by late October he was darting gaily around the kitchen and bumping his head against the ceiling.

A trip I made that fall saved the little traveler thousands of wingbeats. I was going a hundred miles down the Atlantic coast, so I took him with me. At sunset, near a quiet stretch of woods, I opened his cage. He blinked a quick good-by and, looking pitifully small, flew off to a tangle of cat brier.

In imagination I followed him on his trip, seeing the world through his eyes, but cold terror stopped me as I rehearsed the perils: sleet storms, blinding fog, poison sprays, and predators. The odds were overwhelmingly against him; only sheer luck plus the compelling urge to migrate could carry that wisp of feathers safely to his winter home.

Yet I hoped that he might make it and return again in the spring with his clan to feed on the caterpillars that infest our forests. For by an ingenious arrangement of nature, he and his close relatives, the bright-feathered wood warblers, protect our trees. At every stage of trees' growth, hordes of insects attack them and, if unchecked, would destroy them. Traveling through the woods and orchards, these lively warblers scan the leaves and bark in their unending search for food. They peer for wood borers, bark beetles, and insect eggs; they chase gnats and caddis flies or snap up leaf-hoppers, cankerworms, gypsy-moth caterpillars, and tent caterpillars. Once in a while they may nibble a few berries, but they devour tons of chewing, sucking, boring enemies of trees.

These rainbow-tinted birds are always a delight to the eye but during their spring mating time they really put on a show. Then, in gay wedding finery, hundreds of thousands of these little guardians of the forest pour up the East and West coasts like waves breaking on a beach. More than fifty different kinds of wood warblers come from South America, Cuba, and Mexico to lay their eggs in the United States and Canada and gladden the hearts of bird-watchers.

Scratch a bird-watcher and you are likely to find a warbler fan, here in the East anyway. In the West the warblers drift in over a longer period and without spectacular flights, but in states east of the Mississippi "birding" excitement comes to a boil during the big northward push of wood warblers in the spring. Then housewives neglect their chores and commuters get up before dawn to gaze at these colorful little birds. Even in New York City an early-rising group of warbler buffs, headed by a famous naturalist, prowls the byways of Central Park, long a haven for tired warblers following the northeastern flyway. Fanning out all over, the migrants stop to rest and feed in parks, gardens, woods, and orchards. After two or three weeks, they move on to their more secluded nesting grounds in the deep forests. No other bird clan flies more in mixed company—on some spring mornings twenty-five kinds of warblers can be seen in one area.

## BIRD AMBULANCE

This warbler migration has long puzzled naturalists. By banding nestlings they have found that warblers born in the western states return there, while southern warblers always breed in the deep South. New England birds go back to New England, and Canadian-born warblers always lay their eggs in Canada. Why? And how can each baby warbler step out of its shell carrying in its tiny brain a compass and a built-in sextant that will take it all the way to a distant winter home it has never seen? Experts are still arguing these questions, but they do agree that birds use the sun as a guide in their daytime flights and at night are guided by the stars.

Reassuring themselves with faint lisps and chirps, the tiny warblers travel mostly in the dark at a height of 1000 to 2000 feet. But when bad weather lowers the cloud ceiling, they have to fly blind, like airplane pilots, and closer to the ground. On some misty nights, hundreds crash against the dazzling lenses of Barnegat Light on the New Jersey coast. Buffeted by the wind against the granite shaft of the Washington monument, dozens of little warblers suffer concussions. One morning more than three hundred bruised or dying warblers were scattered on the New York sidewalk below the fog-shrouded Empire State Building. Yet drawn by some instinct, they follow the same ancient flyways each spring, as they swarm north to mate and rear their young. Then, after a few months, back they go to the lands of warmth and sunshine.

Though the wood warblers nest in the temperate zone, their vivid tints show that they are a tropical tribe. Among some kinds the males are brighter than their mates; among others, the sexes look nearly alike. So thinly feathered that they cannot stand much cold, many lose their lives in unseasonable sleet storms during their flights to and from the tropics.

In one of his letters, Theodore Roosevelt, a tireless bird-watcher, reported seeing a strange bird in a tree on the White House lawn in May. It was a tiger-patterned bird with chestnut cheeks and a bright yellow breast, which a naturalist identified as a Cape

May warbler. Like our twenty-sixth President, eastern bird-watchers look for warblers in parks and woodlands during the month of May. In spite of their name, the warblers' songs are not very musical; they often sound like "wheezy, wheezy, wheezy" but these buzzy little trills help to locate them in the trees.

About the first to arrive in our home-town oaks are the fairly common myrtle warblers, one of the few warblers that can live on berries and seeds. In fact, the black-and-white-streaked myrtle gets its name from a favorite berry, although in spring it too feeds on caterpillars and plant lice. As the myrtles dart among the lower branches, you can see their lemon-colored wing and rump patches even without fieldglasses.

Hunting insects, a golden bird, bright as a canary, sometimes flies around the shade trees in streets and parks. It is the yellow warbler, a clever little bird that often solves an unusual problem with Spartan courage. The much bigger cowbird, an unnatural mother who doesn't raise her own children, likes to lay her eggs in this warbler's nest. When she does, the warbler weaves a new bottom over her own eggs as well as the cowbird's egg, burying them all so none will hatch. (If they did, the baby cowbird would crowd the young warblers out of their tiny cradle.) Then the yellow warbler lays another clutch of eggs. Again and again the cowbird may come back and the warbler work to foil her. In one amazing case, a six-storied nest was found with a cowbird's egg in every layer.

For most bird-watchers, the coming of the warblers has the same effect as catnip on a cat. Last spring a friend stopped me, frantically waving his binoculars.

"Parulas, parulas, flocks of them in the woods today," he alerted me.

To a warbler fan, this outlandish name means the smallest warbler found in the East—4¼ inches of blue and yellow feathers.

# BIRD AMBULANCE

(For comparison, the length of an English sparrow is figured as 6 inches.)

That afternoon I took to the woods where other bird-watchers were already comparing notes. But something must have changed the warbler timetable; though they were undoubtedly on the wing all the way from the Gulf of Mexico to the Gulf of St. Lawrence, I didn't see one. After three hours in the woods my neck ached from looking up at the trees and I finally left without having seen anything more exciting than  a pair of crows. Then, coming back home, I spotted in my own shrubbery a bouncy little yellow-throat. This peppy member of the warbler clan sports a yellow bib and black domino mask. A very useful bird, it has been given credit for saving many a pear orchard from infestations of the psylla pest.

In Maine I had the greatest thrill a warbler fan can know. On a trip to Bar Harbor, I was strolling through the famous Reef Gardens. There was a flash of orange feathers against some spruces as a small bird dipped to the ground. Dropping to my knees, I inched toward it under a tangle of evergreens. For a moment I had a full view—black back, white wing bars, brilliant orange-to-peach breast and head. "Blackburnian!" I caught myself whispering.

A naturalist with a touch of the poet called this bird "Prometheus, the Torch-bearer," and, backed by the dark branches, its throat did shine like a tongue of fire as it moved into a ray of sunlight. Scrambling up and brushing my clothes, I was too pleased with my luck to mind the amused looks of other visitors who had watched me crawling around under the trees. At last I had seen that prize beauty of the warbler family.

Though the Blackburnian is undoubtedly the showiest, some warbler enthusiasts think the redstart is the most appealing. The Cubans have a special name for this heart-stealer from the West Indies—*candelita* (little torch). They call the other warblers *mariposas* (butterflies). The restless male redstart, black with flame-colored wing and tail patches, sometimes drops down to a handy birdbath after a hard day of hunting spittle bugs and leaf hoppers. His mate, in softer colors—olive with yellow markings—is likely to wait timidly nearby. They stay only a moment before taking off to some quiet woodland to make a jewel case for their gemlike eggs.

Warblers' nests are often exquisite confections, designed of dream-stuff materials. Milkweed floss, deer's hair, downy fern fronds, flowers, and feathers are used for lining. Bits of moss or rabbit's tobacco, deftly fastened with caterpillar silk, at times decorate the outside.

One of the most fanciful nest builders is an eye-catching western bird with an orange head, the olive warbler. Breeding in Arizona, she lays her green-and-sepia eggs in a delicate cup lined with fir blossoms and rootlets. Studded with lichens, the outside is cunningly woven of spiders' gossamer. The parula's nest, however, is an exception. This happy-go-lucky little warbler merely turns up an end of old man's beard moss (Usnea) to make a pocket for her tiny eggs.

The colorful warbler clan is very numerous now. A billion is a conservative guess. During the summer months, about every sixth bird in the United States is a wood warbler, and in the deep forests of Canada, they make up more than half the nesting songbirds.

Unfortunately a dark shadow clouds their future in the shape of hovering helicopters spraying poisons to control that forest pest the gypsy moth. Since the caterpillars of this moth make up a good part of the warblers' diet, poisoning their food may eventually kill off these delicate birds. Ironically, insects like the gypsy moth soon build up an immunity to the poisons which is passed on to their offspring; with fewer warblers to eat them, this pest can increase rapidly, requiring an even stronger spray.

Ecologists now believe that a more sensible approach to the gypsy-moth problem is the introduction of its natural, parasitic enemies—insects that themselves will destroy the moth. This method has already been tried with good results. Such scientists insist the ultimate control of insects must be biological, not chemical, if our wildlife is to survive.

Hopefully, an aroused public will put a stop to the unwise practice of drenching the forests with poison sprays. If so, the sequences of nature can go on as usual: feeding on the caterpillars that eat the budding leaves, the colorful wood warblers move north just when the insects hatch. Spring arrives, the warblers return, and bird-watchers are ecstatic.

# 9

## PIGEON IN RESIDENCE

*Limpy*

# 9. Pigeon in Residence

EVERY morning as I am preparing breakfast, a visitor comes to my window—a slate-blue bird with an iridescent throat. It's Limpy, my stiff-legged pigeon.

Almost six years ago on a chilly April day, an anxious woman arrived holding a cat carrier. In it, rolled in a towel, was a week-old pigeon with a bleeding leg. She had found it in the hollow of a subway grating.

"Some people don't like pigeons," she said apologetically, "but this is a living creature and I just couldn't leave it to die."

How it got in the grating was a mystery. There were no buildings nearby from which it might have fallen and it was much too young to walk. Besides being the youngest pigeon I had ever handled, it was also the dirtiest. Its yellowish down and overly large beak were caked with mud and soot. Cold and weak, it had obviously been without its pigeon "milk" for some time, since its little crop was quite empty.

When a pigeon is first hatched, it can hardly lift its head. Gaining strength, it nuzzles feebly at a parent, which then opens its mouth for the youngster to slip its beak into its throat. Then the pigeon "milk," a cream-colored curd formed in the crops of both parents, is regurgitated into the baby's mouth. The cock pigeon is the only male vertebrate that produces a milk for his young; the hen pigeon the only feathered female that does so. Scientists have no explanation for this phenomenon which occurs only in the pigeon family.

Pigeons have been man's companions since biblical times, so hand rearing them by using a substitute for this "milk" has gone on for quite a while. Arrowroot flour mixed with milk, or infant cereals such as pablum, have been used. A modern substitute is well-moistened Gaines meal laced with a beaten raw egg. These pellets of meal, made of ground corn, soybeans, and wheat middlings, seem to agree with young pigeons and doves of all ages. When the bird is very young, the mixture must be as thin as a watery gruel. Later it can be thickened a bit.

Whatever the formula, it is a messy process to administer, the trick being to open the youngster's beak with one hand and insert some of the runny mixture with the other. The first time I fed Limpy, I got more on the outside than on the inside. To avoid washing him so often, I made him a bib of a scrap of plastic. He quickly learned the bib meant food, and as soon as he saw it, he began flapping his stumpy wings and squeaking "Peent, peent, peent," all the while running around in circles as he tried to nuzzle my fingers. Then when he was about six weeks old, I folded his bib for the last time and put it away; Limpy could now eat out of a dish.

At first he pecked the moistened dog-food pellets, later wild-bird seed, grit, and pigeon food. By then he was living in the outside shelter with my other birds and taking practice flights across the room. But one morning I found him beating his wings against the screen, so I concluded he wanted to leave. As there is always a flock of pigeons in a nearby park, I released him there, hoping he would join them. But he never did; he still roosts in the oaks in my yard and with his stiff-legged gait patrols the garden, picking up crabgrass and weed seeds and an occasional sow bug. Except for the handful of grain I give him in the morning, he does his own foraging. One year he seemed to have a mate, a ginger-colored pigeon who stayed with him for a season. But she disappeared; perhaps it was a mutual-consent separation.

Over the years, Limpy has become such a fixture that I hardly noticed his comings and goings, until one day a neighbor, a professor of oriental languages at a nearby college, dropped by to see the birds. He drew my attention to the familiar pigeon on the window ledge. After I finished giving him Limpy's history, he remarked, "When I was a boy in Peking before the Janapese invasion, pigeons were my hobby."

As he enlarged on the subject, I listened enthralled, hearing for the first time about the custom of attaching flutes to the tails of oriental pigeons, which fill the air with music as the birds fly about. Made of bamboo or reed, these flutes are naturally very light, about ⅛ ounce, and are attached to the two middle tail feathers. These feathers are sewed together with thread, about ¼ inch from the body, then the bone handle at the base of the flute is pushed between the tail feathers, where it is held in place by a small wire ring.

"Pigeon fanciers in Peking greatly prized those flutes," my neighbor concluded. "They weren't easy to come by—only five families in all the city knew how to make them and they kept their methods secret."

My knowledge of pigeons and their fascination for people increased by leaps and bounds after reading a beautifully illustrated book entitled *The Pigeon* by Wendell Mitchell Levi, which the professor was kind enough to lend me. Pigeons belong to the same family as doves, which are mentioned in Genesis; it was a dove that brought tidings of land to Noah after the flood. At first Noah sent out a raven, but it failed to return; then he sent out a dove which brought back an olive leaf.

The most dramatic part of pigeon history has to do with their role in war. For centuries pigeons were used by the military as a means of liaison and have proved faithful couriers. Men on horseback and runners were slow in comparison with these feathered messengers. Although with all our modern inventions pigeon messengers might be expected to have become obsolete, in World War One, World War Two, and the Korean War, they played a vital part. When telephone or telegraph wires were cut or tapped, the intelligent and well-coordinated homing pigeon often was able to get through to headquarters with important information.

Until the end of World War Two, many boys and men in the suburbs kept pigeons as a hobby. Then, with increasing urbanization, zoning became stricter, often prohibiting the building of lofts or poultry houses. Sometimes pigeon fanciers moved away from their old neighborhoods and, because of restrictions in their new locations, had to give up their pets. Rather than destroy them, they let them go free. As a result, over the years flocks of pigeons have gravitated to city parks, where lonely people, deprived of pets, take pleasure in feeding and watching them. Needing only a little protection and shelter, these "common pigeons" build their nests in niches and the gable openings of buildings, which their droppings often deface. Many owners, understandably annoyed, have branded the pigeons as nuisances. They prod the Board of Health officers into making statements that pigeons are disease carriers and should be exterminated. But pigeons have been raised for too many centuries by too many millions without any trace of health impairment to successfully incriminate them as disease bearers. Although periodically there are scares fanned by writers for publicity, not one case has been found where it was actually proved that pigeons are disease carriers and injurious to public health.

Pigeon detractors point to them as an ever-increasing nuisance; pigeon defenders argue that they are one of the few humanizing relics left in our all-too-dehumanized cities. In line with the modern trend is a new humane way to cut down the surplus pigeon population. A chemical now on the market causes temporary sterility (for about six months)—a sort of birth-control pill for pigeons. The birds are fed whole kernels of corn coated with this chemical. As the older birds die off and no baby pigeons are hatched, by attrition the flocks grow smaller. Whole kernel corn is used because it is too big to be eaten by songbirds. By the use of this chemical control from 1967 to 1970, a flock of 2500 pigeons in Bangor, Maine, was reduced to about 300 after two years.

For best results the treated corn should be scattered in early spring and fall, under the supervision of government agencies or conservation groups. It should be distributed on rooftops, bell towers, and all traditional pigeon feeding locations but not in areas used by waterfowl or other corn-eating birds. Perhaps this method of solving the population explosion of vagrant pigeons will be acceptable to pigeon detractors and pigeon defenders alike.

# 10

## "DEAR ABBY"

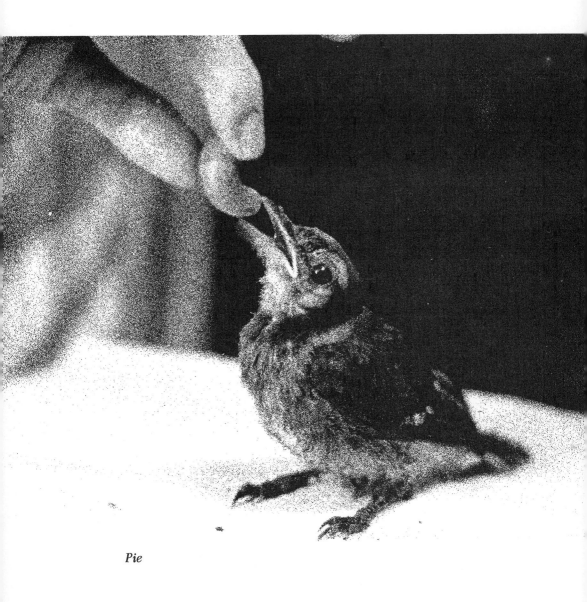

*Pie*

# 10. "Dear Abby"

HERE in the suburbs where birds co-exist so closely with people, perplexing situations often arise. From the questions I am asked during the year, I sometimes think a Dear Abby column for birds would be popular.

Once a concerned suburbanite telephoned to learn the identity of a bird nesting in her shrubbery that sang at intervals all night. Not that she minded, but its outbursts so disturbed her neighbors by waking their baby that they were threatening to "get" it. My first guess was a mocking bird, which often practices its songs on moonlit nights. But she described the bird as smaller than a sparrow and played over the telephone a recording that she had made of its song. From the size, and the lilting gurgles repeated at short intervals, I was convinced that the bird was a wren. I felt fairly safe in assuring her that, after its young were hatched, it would be too busy filling their hungry little mouths to indulge in any more sleep-wrecking serenades. I hoped she could convince her neighbor of this, and presumably she did, since she never called back to report that the threatened assassination had taken place.

Then there is the perennial report that "ferocious" blue-jays are attacking people. This has become such a common notion that the New York Zoological Society has printed a statement to the effect that suburbanites should not be frightened by these birds' defense of their nests. People are advised to stay away from the vicinity of the jays' nests or, if that is impossible because a nest is near a public walk, to pay no attention to the darting fluttering birds. They will not hurt anybody.

Every summer people are confronted with the knotty problem of bird-killing cats, one not always easy to solve. In New York and many other states songbirds, as well as most other birds, are "protected." This means it is against the law to harm them, their young, or their eggs at any time. When fledgling birds leave the nest, they flutter to the ground and for several days can only make weak little flights. With a bird-killing cat on the powl, it is a time of great peril for these youngsters and of much apprehension for bird lovers. I try to have this explained to cat owners, and many do co-operate by keeping cats indoors or else putting them out on a leash. Some, however, contend that their cats have a "right" to hunt. I inform such people of Section 186 of the New York State Conservation Law, which few of them had dreamed exists:

"Any person over the age of 21 years possessing a hunting license may, and game protectors and peace officers shall, humanely destroy cats at large found stalking or killing a protected wild bird or with a dead bird of any protected species in its possession."

Recently a frantic woman called about an unconscious robin she had fished out of her lily pool. "Hold it upside down to get the water out of its lungs and then try to warm it," I suggested, without much hope of her succeeding. An hour later she called back. She had resuscitated it by breathing into its mouth and flapping its wings, and the bird was now calmly preening itself.

About the middle of May, when people get ready to turn on their air conditioners, they often find that birds (especially starlings and sparrows) are using them for nesting boxes. "What shall we do?" they inquire. I explain that the young birds leave the nest about two weeks after hatching and, once gone, will not come back. Many kind-hearted home owners patiently count the days until they can take possession of their air conditioners. Then they usually screen any openings so another bird tenant cannot move in.

Picture windows are another hazard of suburbia. Not noticing the glass, birds sometimes think the house is an extension of the garden and crash into the window. One way to prevent this is to hang draw curtains across the windows: even thin, gauzy ones help. A better plan is to stretch some sheer material across the outside of the panes. Of course the material will have to be renewed every year or so, but considerate people are glad to do this if it saves the lives of many birds.

"After they're released, can birds raised by people get along in the wild?" is a frequent question. Like those reared by their natural parents, some do, some don't. Since two-thirds of all young birds hatched in a year die before the following spring, the mortality rate is very high. However, it is encouraging to learn that one woman banded a bird she had reared and for three successive springs it returned to her garden.

One thing I feel sure of: too long dependency in hand-raised birds can be a serious detriment. Very young birds stretch their necks, open their mouths, and flutter their wings, a behavior pattern called "begging." Ordinarily this infantile practice stops soon after the young birds leave the nest, generally when they are three or four weeks old for passerines. The growing-up process is encouraged by the parents, who gradually ignore the youngsters' begging, a form of weaning that forces them to pick up their own food. With hand-reared birds, too much coddling and prolonged hand feeding delays the day of independence.

A case in point was a young blue jay that a couple had found in their yard. It had been crippled in infancy, and its legs were so twisted that it could not stand up. It probably fell or was pushed out when the time came for it to leave the nest. This crippling among young birds seems to be increasing, and biologists are raising the question whether it may not be another side effect of the poisoned insect sprays. Whatever the cause, massive doses of Pervinal—eight to nine drops per day—work wonders, often resulting in complete recovery.

This particular foundling, which its rescuers christened Pie, had responded nicely to the Pervinal treatment. Even when full grown, however, it was still begging for food and being hand fed. Then the couple had to go away for a month.

"Would you care for it until we get back and can release it in its home territory?" they asked me.

Knowing how hard it sometimes is for a newcomer to be accepted in the bird world, I agreed. While the jay was staying with me, I fed it by hand only two or three times a day and gave it no special attention. As a result it quickly learned to pick up its own food. One of its idiosyncrasies was a passion for cashew nuts. Another was its friendship for an amiable female rabbit that was living temporarily in the bird shelter. After its daily bath, the jay dried itself on her fur and used her back for a perch, while he jabbered softly to her. This went on for several days, but when I caught him poking cashews into her long ears, I had to step in and end the affair.

When the solicitious couple returned, their jay, although it still had one crooked toe, was eating and flying so well that it was ready to be taken home and released. But, worried about its survival in the wild, its benefactors first put it in their spare bedroom, made birdproof with sheets of cellophane. Later they tried to shoo it out to the yard where it had been born. By that time, the bird would have none of this and retreated to a high valance over a window. Here it spent the day, screaming at the woman, as jays do so well, and snatching its food on the wing.

In consultation, we decided that the best course was to put some food on the outside of the window, then, when the bird started to eat, to slip behind it and slam the window. This strategy did not work, and besides, the couple were afraid the bird might get hurt if it should try to scramble back into the room when the window dropped.

Finally they decided to leave its food outside altogether, hoping it would eventually get the urge to eat and go. But the jay continued to sit on the valance, seeming to prefer starvation to life in the outdoors. At last in desperation they opened the window from the top and went outside where they hoisted a basketful of mouth-watering cashews at eye-level with the valance. Ultimately the hungry bird made a dash for the basket, and the man slapped a screen across the window, barring its return.

Then the couple began to worry. Could a bird apparently so fond of the indoors survive outside? Would it find enough food and be accepted by its kind? They even considered luring it back and turning the bedroom over to it for the winter.

In time I heard the outcome. Not only did the bird, easily identified by its bent toe, survive, it has been unconditionally accepted by the neighborhood jays. Every day, as it raids the nut supply kept available in a basket outside its former bedroom, it brings with it a noisy blue gang, all of whom are now madly addicted to cashews.

This jay was a case of prolonged infancy due to over-solicitude, but birds raised by humans should not be released too soon either. If they are, they may be bewildered by their new surroundings and not find food soon enough—always a life-and-death matter in the wild. After one of my hand-raised fledglings has been eating by itself for a few days, I put it out in the enclosed shelter, where there is a dish of food, and then ignore it as much as possible. Gradually the tame little bird that used to perch on my head or shoulder begins to avoid my hand. By the time I feel it is ready to be given its freedom (usually two or three weeks after it has been on its own in the shelter), I often have to catch it with a net in order to release it.

Birds that live in flocks, such as sparrows, starlings, grackles, and finches, stand a better chance of being accepted by their kind at any season of the year than do those that adhere to strict territorial rights, such as robins, thrushes, bluebirds, and thrashers. If possible, I prefer to release the hand-reared fledglings of such territorial birds in late summer, when the young are more readily accepted because the adults are already on the move toward their winter homes.

This applies to the small perching birds most often found in our gardens. However, birds of prey, such as hawks and owls, stay with their parents longer since they have to learn much about the fine art of hunting. Practice with falling feathers, a piece of cardboard dragged along on a string, or paper balls thrown on the floor is a good way to teach these birds to snatch at moving objects. Still better is the method used at the Audubon camp for my baby owls, who learned to hunt in a field of lively grasshoppers.

# 11

## SWIFTS IN THE CHIMNEY

*Swifts three*

# 11. Swifts in the Chimney

A WEEK before wreckers tore down a Long Island farmhouse, its human tenants moved out. But when the old brick chimney crumbled, three other tenants were evicted without notice. Picking the bright-eyed waifs out of the rubble, one of the crew determined to save them if possible. After telephoning around for help, he drove twenty-seven miles to bring them to me.

Though their coal-black feathers looked glossy and healthy and their chittering call was strong, when I saw the little chimney swifts, my heart sank. I had failed in an earlier attempt to rear these odd birds that fasten their nests in unused silos and chimneys and raise their young in near darkness. At that time I did not know a good substitute for their diet of winged insects.

This time I decided to try the formula used for swallows and flycatchers: scraped lean beef with vitamins. (Chopped beef is not as nourishing, I am told, and may be fatty.) For extra pep, I added mashed egg yolk, unflavored gelatin, and dried flies.

Besides finding a substitute diet for them I had to improvise a substitute chimney, for they cling by their feet in a vertical position even in the nest. This twig nest is in the shape of a triangle. While constructing it, the parents hold a small bundle of sticks against the wall by their stiff tail feathers. One by one the sticks are taken up, covered with saliva, and stuck in place. The saliva looks like glycerin and after drying is surprisingly strong.

Each of the many different swifts in the world—some sixty kinds in all—has a distinctive nesting site and material. The little gray-rump that lives in the Malaya and Indo-China even makes a nest "good enough to eat." A cup-shaped concoction, this is constructed solely of a protein-rich saliva that the bird glues in a cave or on the side of a cliff. This is the nest used to make that centuries-old oriental treat, a delicious consommé known the world over as birds'-nest soup. Quantities of these little nests, having a market value of a hundred thousand dollars or more, are gathered each year by the natives. Using bamboo ladders, the collectors knock the nests down as soon as the birds finish making them. The swift usually has enough saliva left to build a second nest, but if that one is also taken, the third nest is often too flimsy to hold the young birds.

When the nest of our native chimney swift is only half-finished, egg laying begins. Both parents keep on with the nest building during the laying period and stop just before the eggs hatch. Although their nest is only a basket of sticks and saliva, it is nicely suited to the young swifts' needs. Their nails are well developed at hatching and the twig nest has many places to grip. Unlike swallows, these birds are unable to perch since their legs are mere stumps ending in four tiny claws with sharp nails.

But to compensate for this deficiency, the swifts in their own way have become kings of flight. Eons ago their wings developed at the expense of their legs, as their classification, the *apodiformes*, or footless ones, implies. Characteristic of this order are the wing bones: The upper one, the humerus, is short and stout, the thin, pointed wing being formed mainly by the long bones growing from beyond the "elbow," which give the flying muscles better leverage.

These aptly named birds are all extremely fast on the wing, many averaging as much as 100 miles an hour. The speediest is the spine-tail, a fantastic flyer that has been clocked going 200 miles per hour.

I put my fledglings in a high wicker basket, the side of which they could grip in about the same way as they had clung to their original twig nest. They quickly settled themselves in their new home, and I began scraping beef which I pushed into their wide mouths hourly. Their bills are tiny, but their gape is large and allows them, when flying, to inhale such food as flies, midges, and other air-borne insects. They soon got to know my step and began their chittering before I reached their basket. When really hungry, they sounded like a dozen sewing machines going full blast.

The sudden arrival of the three little chimney swifts had me digging for every scrap of information published about these often-seen but little-known birds. Studying photographs made by one authority, I estimated that mine were about eighteen days old when I got them. At this age they have normally crawled out of the nest and are climbing around in their natal chimney but not yet ready to fly out.

In about a week my birds had had enough of their basket and would scramble out whenever I lifted the cover. So I put them in my outside shelter where rehabilitated birds can try out their wings before they are released. Clinging to its screened sides, they created quite a sensation among visitors, who usually thought they were bats until I explained their habits. Impressed but confused, one youngster told his mother I had three chimney sweeps at my house. Understandably she concluded that I was entertaining some professional soot removers from England.

As their wings lengthened, the fledgling swifts seemed to do definite exercises. With bodies tipped forward and tail spread, they violently flapped their long slender wings, a preparation no doubt for aerial flight, which once begun, rarely stops. Their flying is so effortless that they need little rest and, once launched, are credited with spending the entire night on the wing. Young swifts do not leave the nest until they are ready for sustained flight, for if one fluttered to the ground it might not be able to take off again. Probably because they do postpone their departure from the nest until their wings are very strong, banding statistics show that young swifts escape the high first-year death rate of many other fledgling birds.

Since there were no parent birds to teach my foundlings, the question of how they would learn to take food from the air bothered me. But a section from *Swifts in a Tower* by David Lack, an authority on these birds, was reassuring:

"Eventually the time comes for the nestling swift to depart. Until now, its knowledge of the outside world has been only what it could see by looking out of the entrance hole; afterward it will not return to its nest, it will have nothing more to do with its parents and it will fend entirely for itself. Nearly all the young studied have left when their parents were out hunting and were unaware the nest would be empty when they return. Thwarted in their urge to feed their young, the parents usually sit facing the entrance and make swallowing movements or leave with the food in their mouths, returning to the roost for several more days, but their fledglings are never seen again. There is perhaps no more striking instance in birds of the efficiency of inborn behavior than this of the young swift, which, after its cramped life in the nest enters on its air-borne life in a very wide world, feeds itself, finds some way of spending the night and migrates, all without help from its parents."

Because of their practice of nesting in chimneys, I decided that the birds should be launched from a place as high as possible. So one August morning I put them in their substitute chimney, carried it to an attic window, and opened the screen.

Clinging to the edge of their basket, they looked out over the rooftops, their dark eyes glinting with apparent excitement at their first unobstructed view of the outside world. After a while they stretched their wings and preened a little, alternately fluffing and flattening their body feathers. Balanced on the basket's rim, they looked like oversized butterflies as they slowly opened and closed their dark, slender wings. Suddenly two of them took off, flying high over a stand of oaks, and disappeared.

The third one hesitated, then shrank back in the basket. There it sat for a while, feeling, I imagined, some of the stresses of a parachute jumper getting ready to take his first plunge. But, confidence returning, it edged toward the opening again, teetered a second, and launched itself, following with assurance the same path as the others.

Holding the empty basket, I wondered at their purposeful flight into a world until then wholly unknown. How would they fare on their long trip to the rain forests of the Amazon where they must go to spend the winter? But I trusted the instinct of migration that has safely guided countless birds to their ultimate destination. As far as my crescent-winged trio was concerned, I told myself it would not fail.

# 12 ~

## EXTENDING A HELPING HAND

*A strawberry box full*

# 12. Extending a Helping Hand

ALTHOUGH nursing wild birds is not everyone's cup of tea, there are many ways in which concerned people can help them.

Until the advent of the automobile, few birds lost their lives on old-time gravel or dirt roads. In the horse-and-buggy days an occasional turtle or snake was injured or crushed, but rarely a bird. The first cars, with an average speed of 25 miles per hour, ran down a few rabbits, skunks or roving house cats blinded by their headlights, but there were still not many bird casualties except for chickens. Then came the network of paved highways and the fast cars, resulting in an appalling toll of birds that gets higher every year. During a single day in Florida, state authorities reported that cars killed or maimed 5000 quail, 2000 songbirds, and 250 turkeys, in addition to deer, rabbits, and squirrels.

Another survey in Illinois, made recently by some forest-preserve naturalists on 21,000 miles of highway passing through or bordering wooded areas, showed that birds and mammals killed by traffic were about the same per square mile of land as the annual kill by hunters. For wild creatures, the car has become as deadly as the gun.

## BIRD AMBULANCE

To call attention to and help check this sky-rocketing kill of birds and mammals, a New York organization, Friends of Animals, has printed a bumper sticker reading: WARNING: I BRAKE FOR ANIMALS. At all times, but especially when driving near wooded areas, please be watchful and slow down for birds and other wildlife on the highway.

Another way to help save the lives of birds is to avoid the fad of gardening with poisons. The most lethal of these are the chlorinated hydrocarbons, such as DDT, dieldrin, aldrin, heptachlor, and endrin. These are the long-lived, fat-soluble chemicals that tend to be magnified in natural ecosystems by being passed from one link to another in food chains and thus poison the landscape. The use of these chemicals is now considered the greatest ecological blunder of the generation. Tests made by the California Department of Fish and Game show that 1½ pounds of dieldrin can kill 4 million chicks, as well as any dogs, cats and wild birds that come within its toxic range.

These bird-killing insecticides are so widely accepted that the home gardener is bewildered by the long rows of them in every hardware store, garden-supply shop, and supermarket, and little is done to warn him that he is handling extremely dangerous chemicals. On the contrary, a constant stream of gadgets make it easier and easier to use poisons on lawns and gardens. These chemicals are sold under brand names that never suggest their deadly contents. To learn they contain DDT, dieldrin, or any of the rest, the gardener must read the very fine print on the least conspicuous part of the container. With push-button ease, insecticides fatal to bird and beast can be sprayed onto every bush and tree.

An example of how DDT affected birdlife in one area was observed when Dutch elm disease threatened the campus elms at Michigan State University. The trees were sprayed with DDT to kill the elm-bark beetles which spread this disease. The beetles died, but so did the many robins that nested in the trees. The leaves covered with DDT fell on the ground to become food for earth-worms, which were eventually eaten by the robins. After they had eaten enough DDT-impregnated worms, their DDT levels rose to a point where they died of nerve poisoning. Birds suffer from this more than humans or mammals because they cannot excrete liquids so quickly and the poison accumulates in their bodies. Within a few years robins had disappeared from the area.

After the robins had disappeared from the campus as well as from other sprayed localities in Michigan, the Environmental Defense Fund (organized to fight contamination of the air, water, and land) took fifty-six of that state's cities into federal court to stop the use of DDT on elm trees. Eventually this poison was also banned from mosquito-spray work in Michigan, and now, in spite of the fact that farming is a big industry in that state, Michigan has stopped the sale of DDT entirely. Lately there seems to be a phasing out of this one particular pesticide all over the country; the federal government has recommended cutting off the use of DDT within the next two years. However, other long-lived pesticides can still do a great deal of harm.

Incidentally, "pesticide" is a general term for chemicals used to kill pests. These include insecticides to kill insects, herbicides to kill weeds, and fungicides to kill fungi, molds, rusts, and so forth. However, nothing is a pest in moderation. Only occasional excess numbers make an organism a pest. The object, therefore, is to reduce the population of the pest, not to wipe out every insect in the area. Unfortunately, chemical pesticides do just that, which is a serious matter, since many insects—bees, ladybugs, spiders, praying mantises, to name a few—are beneficial. Most leaf chewing by insects is a constructive part of natural processes. So don't panic; don't spray in anticipation. Use dusts rather than sprays. Use spot treatment; don't broadcast.

Aside from the hazards of cars and pesticides, birds face the constant and desperate need for food. Here people can make a positive contribution to their welfare by setting up an outdoor cafeteria. A bird table in the backyard, erected on a post 5 or 6 feet above the ground, will carry many a hungry bird through the winter. Adding a roof will protect the food in bad weather and installing a cat guard (a piece of metal shaped like a small umbrella) halfway up the post will protect birds as they feed.

The table can be a tray only a foot square or longer. Any flat piece of wood or an old cookie sheet will do. Putting an edging about 2 inches high around three sides will keep crumbs from blowing away. Some people fasten a tray to a windowsill where they can watch the birds feeding from indoors. This has the advantage of not having to go out in deep snow to fill it. Another simple feeder can be made from a sawed-off coconut shell hung from a tree and filled with grain or crumbs.

The Fish and Wildlife Service suggests offering chickadees, titmice, and nuthatches suet, cracked nuts, shelled peanuts, sunflower seeds, and bread crumbs. Fruit and insect eaters, such as mockingbirds, thrashers, catbirds, thrushes, and robins (and of course the ever-present starling), are very happy to get cut-up apples and oranges, currants, raisins, and bread crumbs. For birds that live mostly on seeds—blackbirds, cardinals, and towhees—sunflower seeds, corn, shelled peanuts, and scratch feed are good. Juncos, finches, and sparrows like wild-bird seed, bread, and millet. Woodpeckers, both downy and hairy, and chickadees will take suet and sometimes cracked nuts and corn. Some birds, among them sparrows, juncos, and mourning doves, like to eat on the ground. Scatter crumbs and grain for them below the tray—but watch out for cats, which will often jump a feeding bird.

A thick piece of suet can be tied to a corner of the feeding tray or put in a woven string container, such as the bags sometimes used for onions or flower bulbs. A wire soap rack can also be used but has the disadvantage that a bird's tongue can freeze to the wire in zero weather.

To make another easy and popular bird food, boil 1 cup sugar and 1 cup of water for about 5 minutes. Mix with 1 cup melted fat or bacon grease and cool slightly. Then add bread crumbs, corn meal, and bird seed until the mixture is firm. Pack the result in a tin can. This may be put on its side in the crotch of a tree or on a window sill, taking care that the can is secured so the birds can't knock it down. Cardinals, chickadees, titmice, woodpeckers, and nuthatches seem to love ths kind of food can.

Although winter birdlife does not have the big turnover of spring and summer, it can be active and colorful when the outside is brown and sere; a flashing bluejay or brilliant red cardinal can enliven a dull day.

The presence and visits of winter birds are governed by a few major factors, the greatest of which is food. At this season birds are not busy defending a territory for nesting or protecting their youngsters, so their only concern is day-to-day feeding. Many birds will stay in a small backyard if they find a continuous supply of food and some adequate shelter. This leads owners of feeding stations to count on the visits of certain "regulars"; cardinals are likely to be the earliest, followed by chickadees and nuthatches and later jays. Single birds from species that normally do not winter in the area will try (and sometimes succeed) to winter over near a feeding station.

People who see unhappy-looking ducks huddled in an icy pond on a frigid day wonder what to feed them. Bread is always a handy staple. These birds also welcome cracked corn and lettuce. For a real treat, offer them dog-food pellets of ground corn, soybean meal, and wheat middlings. I have brought starving ducks and shore birds (gulls, rails, and sandpipers) back to good health with these nutritious pellets.

If you begin feeding birds in winter, naturalists advise doing so every day. A bird's temperature is about 110 degrees and it needs a lot of food to maintain its body heat. If it becomes dependent on the food you supply, it may not be able to stand a sudden drop in temperature without its daily quota. Certainly the suet and seeds at a feeding station save many a bird's life. It is wiser *not* to start a feeding tray in the fall unless it can be stocked with food daily all winter. Such a bird cafeteria may attract birds that might go other places in cold weather. If suddenly, in the middle of winter, the trays are not filled, some of those birds may suffer and even die. Before putting up a tray, make arrangements to keep it stocked all winter.

Water is a "must" for birds all year round. In winter, when most water is frozen, they particularly welcome a drink. One way to give birds water in cold weather is to put an automatic water warmer in your birdbath. This is a rustproof rod with a cord that plugs into an electric outlet. Thermostat-controlled, it allows electricity to be used only when needed. Carried by nurseries and seed stores, this novel gadget will let birds sip and dip all through the frigid season.

The landscaping around a house can be of help to birds too. Trees, shrubs, and vines are important to birds, but open spaces are needed also. Openings allow the sun to reach the plants and give them luxuriant growth, increase their crops of fruits and seeds, and give more pasturage for insects, thus adding to the birds' food supply.

Large trees, clumps of shrubbery, luxuriant vines, and thick grass combine to make a yard where birds can thrive. Elms, which produce the earliest crop of tree seeds, are spring cafeterias for goldfinches and purple finches. Larches and pines attract crossbills, and red cedar, a tall narrow evergreen, provides food for cedar waxwings, as well as being a good nesting tree for other birds. Oaks and beeches bring woodpeckers and jays, especially in winter; acorns and beechnuts are useful also to grackles, nuthatches, crows, and game birds. Autumn olive, with its attractive pink berries in the fall, provides food for over forty different species, including the cocky mockingbird.

Feeding fruit-eating birds is easily done by planting fruiting shrubs and trees. Through late spring and summer there are enough insects in addition to fruit for all the birds. Fall is the season of abundance in fruit; in winter the supply dwindles and in late winter there is often a scarcity. Fortunately, everywhere in the United States there are some fruits that last until there is no longer need for them, and if enough of these trees and shrubs are planted, no birds that can live on this kind of food should starve. The best of these long-persisting fruits are those of juniper, hackberry, thorn apple, mountain ash, holly, Virginia creeper, sour gum, snowberry, and bush honeysuckle. Chokeberry, both red and black, and bayberry provide food for warblers, swallows, and quail.

Hooked on hummingbirds? Plant morning glories, petunias, bee balm, salvia, and honeysuckles. Jewelweed, a flower that will grow from Newfoundland to Florida, and trumpet creeper attract these vivid-colored little birds. In California the silk oaks (*Grevillea*) and eucalyptus will have the hummers winging to your yard.

Next in importance to food and water for birds are nesting places to raise their young. Modern tree surgery and the removal of old trees have caused a scarcity of nesting sites for birds that use holes to nest in. Luckily many—flickers, nuthatches, chickadees, some owls, wrens, and bluebirds—will use birdhouses instead. These can be bought from dealers and nurseries or they can be homemade of wood, composition roof shingles or any weatherproof material.

The general idea in building a birdhouse is to have a roof, floor, and walls, and a small "room" inside for eggs. Information about building birdhouses can be obtained from the New York State College of Agriculture and other sources.

Whatever the size of the house, it should have a hinged side or bottom so that it can be easily cleaned. Every spring take out the old nesting material. Gypsy moths and other insect pests sometimes lay their eggs there, and occasionally the house gets infested with bird mites from its former tenants. Dusting the inside of the house wth pyrethrum powder will take care of those unwelcome visitors.

Some birds—robins, phoebes, thrushes, and barn swallows —will not use a covered house but will accept simple shelves or nest brackets with open slides. And some, like the vireos, orioles, bluejays, and hummingbirds, prefer to build their own nests in their own way without any help from outsiders.

At times helping local birds with food and shelter can seem almost futile in the face of the overall threat of pesticides and the destruction of unspoiled woodlands and marshes. For our own well-being, as well as that of our wildlife, some open areas must be left intact.

Many wild birds have endeared themselves to me during their stay at my small-scale bird shelter, where I have had the pleasure of watching little owls play, felt a warbler's clasp, and gained the confidence of a hawk. Hopefully one day a series of permanent shelters will be set up, staffed by professionals, where people can bring these waifs to be nursed back to health, their fate not dependent on scattered volunteers like myself. For my part, I gratefully acknowledge that my ambulance has brought me, along with a variety of patients, a rather special intimacy with those strange, wonderful, and delightful creatures, the birds.

# *INDEX*

*Coco*

# INDEX

feeding birds in winter, 123

feeding young birds, *see* bird care

*Field Guide to the Birds* (Roger Tory Peterson), 3

finch:

Eastern purple (*Carpodacus purpureus purpureus*), 108

house (*Carpodacus mexicanus*), 108

Fish and Wildlife Service, 122

flicker, yellow-shafted (*Colaptes auratus*), 7

food chains, 19

Friends of Animals Society, 120

grackle (*Quiscalus quiscula quiscula*), 108

Griffin, Donald R., 47

Grinnell, George Bird, 5

gull:

Black-backed (*Larus marinus*), 70

herring (*Larus argentatus*), 67

ring-billed (*Larus delawarensis*), 70

hawk:

goshawk (*Accipter gentilis atricapillus*), 78

red-tail (*Buteo jamaicensis*), 75

hummingbird, ruby-throated (*Archilochus colubris*), 6, 125

injured birds, *see* bird care

Jamaica Bay Wildlife Refuge, 69, 81

Johnson, Herbert, 69

kingbird, Eastern (*Tyrannus tyrannus*), 31

Lack, David, 114

laws about birds, 31, 104, 121

Levi, Wendell Mitchell, 97

mockingbird (*Mimus polyglottos polyglottos*), 125

nesting boxes, 125

New York State College of Agriculture, 125

New York Zoological Society, 7, 47, 104

nuthatch, white-breasted (*Sitta carolinensis*), 4

Oil pollution, *see* bird care

owl:

barred (*Strix varia*), 22

great gray (*Strix nebulosa nebulosa*), 22

saw-whet (*Aegolius acadica acadica*), 22

screech (*Otus asio*), 17, 21

pesticides, 106, 120–121

Peterson, Roger Tory, 3, 21

pigeon (*Columba livia livia*):

birth control, 99

flutes, 97

food for young, 96

*Pigeon, The* (Wendell Mitchell Levi), 97

plants to attract birds, 125

praying mantis (*Mantis religiosa*), 39–41

quail (*Colinus virginianus*), 119

*130*

roadkill, 119

robin (*Turdus migratorius*), 28, 30, 121

Roosevelt, Theodore, 88

ruffed grouse (*Bonasa umbellus*), 34

Scott, George, 7, 66

skimmer, black (*Rynchops nigra nigra*), 70

sparrow, English (*Passer domesticus domesticus*), 90, 108

squirrel, gray (*Sciurus carolinensis*), 42–45

starling (*Sturnus vulgaris vulgaris*), 6, 108

Stroud, Robert, 12, 64

swallow, barn (*Hirundo rustica erythrogaster*), 126

swift:
  chimney (*Chaetura pelagica*), 113
  gray-rump (*Collocalia inexpectata*), 112
  spine-tail (*Chaetura*), 113

*Swifts in a Tower* (David Lack), 114

tern, common (*Sterna hirundo hirundo*), 70

thrasher (*Toxostoma rufum rufum*), 108

thrush, wood (*Hylocichla mustelina*), 12, 108

timberdoodle, *see* woodcock

*Torrey Canyon,* 79

turkey (*Meleagris gallopavo*), 119

warbler:
  Blackburnian (*Dendroica fusca*), 90
  Cape May (*Dendroica tigrina*), 88–89
  myrtle (*Dendroica coronata coronata*), 89
  olive (*Peucedramus olivaceus*), 91
  parula (*Parula americana*), 89
  pine (*Dendroica pinus*), 85
  redstart (*Setophaga ruticilla*), 90
  yellow (*Dendroica petechia*), 89
  yellowthroat (*Geothlypis trichas*), 90
  nests, 91

water for birds, 68, 124

whippoorwill (*Caprimulgus vociferus*), 6

woodcock (*Philohela minor*), 32

woodpecker, hairy (*Dendrocopus villosus*), 65–66, 122

wren, house (*Troglodytes aedon*), 103